SHREDDING
THE PUBLIC INTEREST
RALPH KLEIN AND 25 YEARS OF ONE-PARTY GOVERNMENT
KEVIN TAFT

THE UNIVERSITY OF
ALBERTA PRESS

AND

PARKLAND
INSTITUTE

First published by:

The University of Alberta Press
141 Athabasca Hall
Edmonton, Alberta, Canada   T6G 2E8
        and
Parkland Institute
Faculty of Arts, University of Alberta
11044–90 Ave.
Edmonton, Alberta, Canada   T6G 2E1

Printed in Canada   5   4   3   2   1

ISBN 0–88864–295–4

Canadian Cataloguing in Publication Data

Taft, Kevin, 1955–
    Shredding the public interest

    ISBN 0–88864–295–4

    1. Alberta—Politics and government—1971– 2. Alberta—Economic policy.
3. Fiscal policy—Alberta. I. Title.
FC3675.2.T33 1997   971.23'03   C97-910033-X
F1078.2.T33 1997

Printed by Webcom Limited, Toronto, Ontario.
∞ Printed on acid-free paper.
Title page cartoon: Malcolm Mayes, originally published in
the *Edmonton Journal*.

COMMITTED TO THE DEVELOPMENT OF CULTURE AND THE ARTS

The University of Alberta Press gratefully acknowledges the support received
for its publishing program from the Canada Council Block Grant program and
the Department of Canadian Heritage.

CONTENTS

ACKNOWLEDGEMENTS

MANY PEOPLE have encouraged and assisted me with this book, and without naming names I thank you all. Especially, I thank my wife for her steadfast support and enthusiasm.

1
INTRODUCTION

AS I WRITE this at the end of 1996, Albertans have been convinced that the cutbacks of Ralph Klein's government were necessary to conquer runaway public spending. Spending on public programs was 'skyrocketing,' 'soaring,' and 'out of control.' Albertans have also been convinced that this government is 'out of the business of business,' having put an end to private-sector subsidies.

Neither of these beliefs is true.

Through careful manœuvring, the Klein government has achieved astonishing political success. This manœuvring has been far from invisible, but it has escaped widespread exposure and analysis. This book uses publicly available statistics, texts of speeches, original analysis, media quotes, the insights of personal experience, and my network in the government to expose some of the tricks of the political trade executed so well by this government.

Ralph Klein became a cabinet minister of the Alberta government after the provincial election of March, 1989. For the next three and a half years, he was a senior member of the Getty government, a government that steadily and determinedly reduced its level of spending on public programs. It was a government that eliminated the jobs of thousands of provincial public employees; reduced medicare benefits and hospital funding; tightened support to schools, universities and municipalities; and cut benefits to seniors.

As a cabinet minister, Ralph Klein had access to information from the Treasury and other departments describing these cuts, and it is reasonable to assume he discussed and helped plan them in cabinet meetings. He certainly sat in the Legislature as they were described, debated, and enacted.

The cuts of the Getty years are facts of history: Alberta's spending on public programs declined significantly. Spending on public programs in Alberta peaked in the mid-1980s. By the time Don Getty resigned, his government had already reduced spending in Alberta to levels at or below the average for Canadian provinces.

Yet since Ralph Klein became premier in December, 1992, the government has worked hard to tell the public a different story, portraying spending on public services in Alberta as 'literally going through the roof.' It has since cut funding to public services again, severely.

As a result of the Klein cuts, public programs in Alberta, including health care, are now funded at the lowest levels in Canada. Even with the government's 'reinvestment' plans announced in the lead-up to the 1997 general election, real spending per person will likely remain at or below the rates of the poorest Atlantic provinces.

Alberta's financial troubles from 1986 to 1993, which the Klein government set out to repair, can be largely attributed to massive subsidies to the private sector and sharply falling resource revenues. These subsidies began to escalate in the mid-1970s and reached astounding heights in the mid-1980s, far exceeding those of any other province. Subsidies to the private sector during this time have cost the Alberta taxpayer billions more than the province has collected in corporate income taxes. Even today, with a booming economy and one of Canada's largest concentrations of big corporations, the net contribution of corporate income taxes to the Alberta Treasury covers less than two percent of total expenditures.

I believe that the public interest in Alberta has been betrayed. This betrayal operates at many levels, and it has had a terrible cost. Public programs—including health care—have shouldered the blame for financial problems caused by subsidies to the private sector. People have paid with their jobs, their health, their public services, and in some cases with their lives.[1] It is to these people and their families that this book is dedicated.

2

BUILDING TRUST

IN AUGUST 1991, I was hired by Alberta's provincial government to work as a research consultant. For many years I had worked with or near the government in positions ranging from junior manager to cabinet-appointed, high-profile committees.[2] This time, I was to work on a project examining how services to seniors could be managed in the future, as Alberta's population grows steadily older. In comparison to most government projects, it was unusually far-sighted, looking not just at the next few years but at the next two decades, anticipating the time when baby boomers would be seniors.

The report was more than just window-dressing. It had signs of political muscle behind it everywhere: close involvement of a cabinet minister, enough money to do the job well, extensive public input, and a steering committee with senior representatives from many government departments, including Health, Education, Social Services, Treasury, Municipal Affairs, and others. A few months after I was hired, the minister responsible for the project, Roy Brassard, was promoted from Associate Minister of Social Services to the newly created Minister Responsible for Seniors, an indicator of the government's priority for this work.

Seniors' organizations were suspicious of the government's purposes. They were worried that the project was no more than a trumped-up government consultation process designed to give a gloss of public consultation to a hidden agenda of cutbacks. Alberta was running huge annual deficits, and the government was reducing services everywhere. Seniors acknowledged deficits were a problem, but wanted the government to work openly with them to review services. Some were convinced that money could be saved and services improved at the same time.

Gradually the suspicions of seniors' groups were allayed. Roy Brassard and his staff (including me) met repeatedly with them. Often these meetings involved dozens of people representing seniors from around Alberta. I was impressed with Brassard's sincerity and skill. He really was building trust, often on a face-to-face basis with people. We are listening, he would say, and we will work with you to improve services. It was always clear that money was tight, but seniors weren't demanding a wholesale boost to spending. Everyone knew that wasn't in the cards. They just wanted honesty, respect, and sincere concern for their issues.

To hear directly from Albertans we arranged twelve public meetings around the province. They were held in community halls and seniors' centres in small towns and big cities. We worked closely with local groups to promote the events. Nine hundred and seventy people participated. People of all sorts came: concerned children of elderly parents, health-care workers, volunteers, and—of course—seniors themselves. Some were in wheelchairs or using walkers, and some drove many miles and took time from other commitments to participate.

The results of these hearings were added to a huge amount of other information before we started writing the final report. We prepared separate research papers on issues ranging from health and housing to elder abuse and technology. We held intensive meetings with a variety of experts. Angus Reid conducted a $50,000 public-opinion survey on issues concerning seniors, during which 1000 Albertans were interviewed by telephone, and focus groups were held in Medicine Hat and Edmonton. One finding was that most Albertans were opposed to reducing benefits to seniors even if the costs of those benefits should rise; another finding was that people were about evenly split between supporting and opposing a tax increase to maintain support to seniors.

We included in our research an analysis of cost trends. Among the public, even at that time, there was a general impression that costs were rapidly rising. Using internal information provided by Alberta Treasury and other departments, we looked at spending on seniors in Alberta during the preceding several years.

We found that spending on seniors in many areas had been falling since the mid-1980s, sometimes dramatically. In housing it had dropped 14% per senior, in transportation 15%, and in social services, which includes many preventive programs, 31%. In health care, where there was an impression that costs for seniors were soaring, the overall change was barely noticeable. Costs in some areas of health care were up, in others down, and in still others there was little change either way.

For some people the results were a surprise, though certainly not for all. As I will discuss, internal briefing documents prepared by the Treasury and circulated within government show that under the Getty government Alberta had squeezed spending harder for several years than had any other government in Canada.

The figures we prepared were reviewed and confirmed, by Alberta Treasury, among others, and they made their way into the secret first draft of the final report as a relatively short section. Then internal consternation began to grow. If the report admitted costs were falling how could further cuts be made? How would seniors, the public, and the media respond? Wouldn't this information give people a club with which to hit the government? And what about all the changes being proposed by the report? Some people wouldn't like them.

On the other hand, there was no doubt that costs were under control, and Albertans had a right to know this. If people want to make good long-term decisions they need good information, not misguided impressions. Everyone who participated in the planning had been told we would be honest and open. We had a relationship of trust to respect.

Phone calls were exchanged among officials, including me, and confidential meetings were held. Stamping 'Confidential' or 'Secret' on reports only draws greater attention to them, so some copies were disguised to look like garbage by removing their covers and striking bold lines through the first page, as if they were ready for the shredder.

By the time the report was approved by the minister for release, it presented a compromise. The title of the section of the report on costs and government expenditures captured the tone: 'There Should Be Concern But Not Alarm With Affordability.' We included information on falling costs, but under pressure from outside the department, we redrew charts to different scales so that the declines appeared less steep.

We also included camouflage information to divert attention from the points that were causing the most worry. This included misleading though not strictly dishonest information, such as cost trends that didn't account for inflation or population growth, or simplistic projections plotted on charts that made it look as if future costs would skyrocket. Nonetheless, enough information remained in the report that an astute reader could see the truth.

During the summer and autumn of 1992, we wrote the final draft of the report. It was tough but honest despite its compromises, and it recommended ways to manage costs while improving services. It went to the Getty cabinet in the fall of 1992, during the Progressive Conservative leadership campaign that eventually elected Ralph Klein premier. The cabinet mulled the report over and eventually approved its release for December 10. The department arranged to print 2000 copies, each complete with a cover letter signed by the responsible minister, Roy Brassard. Cartons and cartons of the report were delivered by the printer to our offices. A major meeting was arranged by the department with leading seniors' groups to release the report.

Our team felt an exciting sense of democracy-in-action working on this report. The politics of confrontation had been replaced with the politics of cooperation. The seniors who participated felt they were respected, and their tone with the government changed from doubt and suspicion to respect and helpfulness. There were improvements to be made to services, and sacrifices too, and people from all sides had worked together in a way I had seldom seen. I had worked on a number of similar projects before, and in only one other had I seen such a sincere effort at good government.

3

SHREDDING THE

EVIDENCE

DON GETTY announced his decision to retire as premier in August, 1992, and Ralph Klein succeeded him through a leadership vote on December 5.

When he was chosen leader of the Tories and Premier of Alberta, Klein faced a number of serious political problems. Among the most damaging were a series of loan guarantees and other business deals that had gone sour; the generous pensions for members of the legislature; and the provincial government's huge annual deficits and accumulated debt.

The first of these problems Klein overcame with the straightforward promise of 'no more loan guarantees,' a promise that the government broke shortly after their election victory the following June.[3] Klein's government solved the problem of public resentment of MLA pensions by simply cancelling the entire MLA pension plan.

But the third problem, the huge deficits and debt, could not be tackled in a single move. Government expenditures in most areas had declined markedly under Getty's government. Public programs in Alberta were being funded at their lowest levels per capita in years, at or below the average of other Canadian provinces. But Getty's government had kept this decline fairly quiet, still wanting Albertans to believe they were getting 'the best' from their province, an expectation strongly engendered during the Lougheed years. As a result, the public was still under the misconception that Alberta spent far more than other provinces.

The public belief that programs were still rich, reinforced by a strong public opposition to tax increases, left open a whole new strategy for Premier Klein's incoming government. He and his ministers strongly reinforced the mistaken perception that spending was out of control and argued vigorously to cut expenditures. They said they would balance the budget with no tax increases. The public rallied around this idea, and Klein's popularity soared. The Liberal opposition under Laurence Decore had already committed to this same line of argument and so was unable to criticize it. Little did Albertans realize they would end up with the most poorly supported public programs in the country.[4]

It took time for this strategy to take shape. But within a week of Klein's leadership victory, those of us working on the seniors report saw the signs that the politics of image management would shoulder out all other considerations. The release of our report was cancelled even before Klein appointed a cabinet.

At first we hoped this was just to allow the settling in of a new premier and cabinet. But when Klein named his new cabinet, Roy Brassard was dropped as Minister Responsible for Seniors. With his eyes moist with tears but retaining his dignity, Roy

Brassard said farewell to the project staff. The report we had prepared was placed within the responsibilities of a new cabinet position given to Dianne Mirosh, who immediately began to stumble from one issue to the next. Time and again Ralph Klein and his staff intervened to prop her up.

Then, after a delay of several weeks, the order came down to shred all copies of the report. It was deemed by someone at a senior level of government unsuitable for the public to see. So, in the second week of February 1993, we began the thankless task. Day after day a secretary would heft the unopened cartons from the storeroom, through the office to the mail room, where we kept the paper shredder. She would tear open a carton, pull the plastic binding off a copy, and begin feeding several pages at a time into our small paper shredder. After a few dozen copies she would have enough shredded paper to fill a large, black-plastic garbage bag, and after a few days these bags piled up in layers almost to the ceiling. I thought of them as body bags. People from outside the office would comment with curiosity on our exploding mound of waste. We were under strict orders of silence.

When the secretary's hands got tired and sore, I— and others—would help. We would break the boxes' seals and, smelling the new ink and paper, pull off the uncracked bindings and send the years of work to oblivion. There was a nervous tension in the office about keeping track of every copy to make sure they were all destroyed. A few copies, each assigned its own number, had been circulated internally. These were tracked down and sent to their doom.

After two weeks every carton had been opened and emptied, every spine broken, every page shredded, and every bag of shredded paper hauled away. The store room was once again empty, and all evidence of the report was gone. Almost.

A skeleton staff drafted a new report, much smaller than the original, under close political supervision. It was sanitized of any material that might cause problems for the new government and its new strategy. It was released in a low-key manner to seniors' groups. It contained none of the information on falling expenditures nor anything significant about changes or reductions in services. After the delay and various rumours, seniors were justifiably suspicious they were being duped.

4
THE GETTY CUTS

B Y 1 9 9 2 , there was plenty of information circulating within the Getty government that showed spending on most public services had dropped markedly from 1985 levels.

In early 1992, less than a year before Ralph Klein became premier, government financial analysts prepared a briefing package on government spending and finances that was circulated at upper management levels. This work was completely independent from our work on the seniors report. It used the most recent information available.

On pages 16 and 18 you will see two graphs from this package.[5] The graph titled 'Program Expenditure Growth Since 1985–86' compares among the ten provinces spending growth on public services such as health care, education, and social services. It covers fiscal years 1985/86 to 1992/93.

This chart, from an internal government briefing document, shows that Alberta had the tightest controls on spending in Canada throughout the very period the Klein government has claimed costs were out of control. Alberta's spending on public programs grew during this period at easily the lowest rate of all governments in Canada. If the graph had

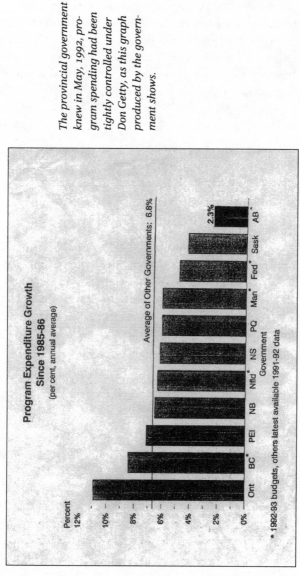

The provincial government knew in May, 1992, program spending had been tightly controlled under Don Getty, as this graph produced by the government shows.

Program Expenditure Growth Since 1985-86
(per cent, annual average)

Average of Other Governments: 6.8%

2.3%

Percent

12%
10%
8%
6%
4%
2%
0%

Ont   BC*   PEI   NB   Nfld   NS   PQ   Man*   Fed*   Sask   AB*

Government

* 1992-93 budgets, others latest available 1991-92 data

accounted for population growth and inflation it would have shown an actual decline in real spending.

The other graph, on page 18, is called 'Health Expenditures in Relation to Other Program Expenditures.' This graph accounts for both inflation and population growth, so it is particularly useful.

This graph offers a direct contradiction to the Klein government's claims of skyrocketing health costs. The line for 'Health' is basically flat from 1986 to 1993, with a slight decline from a peak in 1987.

The reason health care spending takes a bigger piece of today's budget is not because it has gone up, but because other programs have fallen so sharply. The second line covers 'Other Programs,' including areas such as social services, education, environment and transportation. It is clear from this graph that spending in these areas dropped dramatically during the Getty years. The 1993 level is about 23% lower than the 1981 level, and more than 40% lower than the 1986 level.

The Getty government reduced spending in almost every area. This fact may surprise Albertans, but there is much evidence proving it. The work done for the shredded seniors report found this pattern. So did the C.D. Howe Institute, a pro-business think-tank. It ranked Alberta's spending on health care four percent below the Canadian average in 1991 (a result of falling spending in Alberta and rising spending in other provinces).[6]

The Western Centre for Economic Research at the University of Alberta, after studying the government's spending, also found that Alberta's spending fell significantly during Getty's two terms in office:

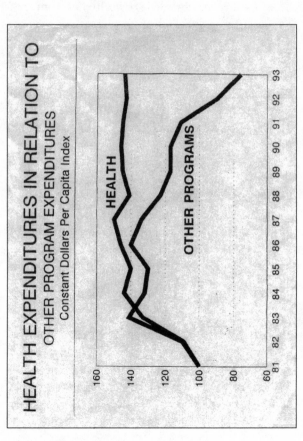

HEALTH EXPENDITURES IN RELATION TO
OTHER PROGRAM EXPENDITURES
Constant Dollars Per Capita Index

HEALTH

OTHER PROGRAMS

160 140 120 100 80 60

81 82 83 84 85 86 87 88 89 90 91 92 93

This government graph clearly contradicts the Klein government's claims of out-of-control spending on public programs from 1987 to 1992.

'Per capita provincial expenditures in Alberta... greatly exceeded those of other provinces during the energy boom but then declined quite markedly from their 1982–83 peak over the following decade.'[7]

● ● ●

You might still find this hard to believe. Memory is a funny thing, and Albertans have been told over and over that costs were rising when the Klein government came to office. We are victims of politically induced amnesia and politically reconstructed history. So here is a quick account of what happened.

Don Getty became premier in October 1985. It was his bad luck that this was the brink of a collapse in oil prices. By August 1986, oil was as low as $10 (US) a barrel, down from a high of over $40 (US) in 1981. The Alberta government's oil and gas revenues fell from $6 billion (Cdn) in 1985 to $2.7 billion (Cdn) in 1987.

As soon as petroleum prices fell, the energy industry began lobbying hard for government breaks, and by the end of the year new and expanded aid packages worth well over $1 billion were announced by Alberta's provincial government.

While assistance to the private sector rose, cuts in public services began within months.[8] In the fall of 1986, newspapers were discussing 'cutback hysteria' as the government struggled to keep its deficit to $3 billion. By early 1987, the Getty government had frozen education spending and doctors' fees, and it had announced plans to cut its own staff by 2000 positions. Spending on capital projects by the province was cut by 14%, and capital spending on schools was chopped in half. Welfare rates were reduced for single, employable persons from $420 per month to $326 per month, and vocational retraining was cut by 26%.

The provincial budget in 1987 continued to cut spending, including reducing student loans and the number of public servants. In interprovincial rankings, Alberta's decline in funding levels was underway, with funding for schools reportedly falling below that of Ontario and Quebec. That autumn, hospitals began to threaten nurses with wage rollbacks to meet reduced budgets.

Even so, massive funds were spent on supporting the energy industry in 1987 (more on this in 'Pulling the Wool' and 'The Spin Doctors,' below). Similarly huge amounts were spent on farmers, who were struggling under low prices, high interest rates, and drought.

In January 1988, a bitter nurses' strike closed many hospitals. When it was resolved, budget restrictions led to reductions in hospital beds and health services. The Alberta Association of Registered Nurses reported a 50% increase in numbers of nurses leaving Alberta. That spring was marked by strikes at schools as the impact of reduced spending began to eat at salaries and working conditions and add to classroom sizes, and through the entire year acrimonious labour negotiations plagued the education system.

In the last half of 1988, the cutbacks slowed and a series of funding announcements prompted *Alberta Report* to call the summer of 1988 the 'Pork-Barrel Summer.'[9] The 'pork' was served widely, with extra portions for the energy industry (including $200 million to help with another 'slump') and agriculture ($850 million in drought relief). Not surprisingly, the halt to cutbacks heralded an election in March 1989, which the Getty government won with a substantial, though reduced, majority.

In 1989 the cuts continued. Doctors had agreed to a new fee pact that constrained their billing, and bed closures and staff cuts continued in health care. Almost half of Alberta's hospitals were running deficits. In July, $110 million was cut from medicare spending. Hospitals began closing beds in summertime to save money.

In 1990, long-term care facilities substantially increased their residents' fees. More hospital beds were closed and more staff were laid off.

Nineteen eighty-nine and 1990 were years of labour confrontation across Alberta. Continuing cuts in school budgets contributed to strikes by teachers and custodians around the province. There were threats of hospital strikes by nurses and support staff, social workers staged illegal walk-outs to protest worsening wages and working conditions, and prison guards walked off the job. In the private sector there were strikes at Suncor and Time Air, as well as by truckers, meatpackers, steelworkers, and pipefitters. A multi-year strike ground along at the Zeidler forest mill.

From 1986 through to the recession that started in 1991, inflation averaged about 5% a year in Alberta, and interest rates varied from about 10% to 14%. This hurt the living standard of many Albertans. It also squeezed government services, for while the high inflation eroded the value of government spending, the high interest rates drove up the cost of borrowing to cover the debt.

In 1991, the general pattern of reduced spending on public services continued, with most provincial government departments struggling to absorb funding cuts. The government implemented an intensified restraint program in November of that year.

From 1990 to 1992 almost 1000 nursing jobs were eliminated province-wide. In 1992 the government negotiated a new funding arrangement with Alberta's doctors to guarantee long-term controls on their billing. The Royal Alexandra Hospital in Edmonton closed one of its CAT-scan machines for lack of funding, and the Minister of Hospitals, Nancy Betkowski, suggested expanding the role of nurses to save money spent on doctors.

Public resentment of these cuts was fuelled by the many subsidies to private industries. In a move that seems symbolic of these, six weeks before handing over the controls to Ralph Klein and six years after the cuts to public services began, the Getty government announced yet another aid program for the energy industry, this one worth $485 million.[10]

The effects of the Getty cuts were sharp and clear. Per capita government spending fell 15%, adjusting for inflation.[11] By fiscal 1991/92, Alberta had dropped from the highest spending of the ten provinces in the early and mid-1980s, to below the Canadian average. The number of provincial employees had declined by the equivalent of 4400 full-time jobs in six years.

In other words, the severe cuts of the Klein government *began* on budgets that were already relatively low. As the government's own chart on page 16 shows, the Getty cabinet, for all its bad publicity, fumbled deals, and lousy luck, had run the tightest government in Canada.

The Getty government took pride in the cuts and was pleased to be leading a government that was steadily getting smaller. With their privileged knowledge of internal government information, members of the Getty cabinet—which included Ralph Klein and future Provincial Treasurer Jim Dinning—would have known just how deep their cuts had gone.

Sometimes the Getty government tried to score political points for its fiscal responsibility. In 1991, Treasurer Dick Johnston stood in the Legislature and spelled out the scale of the cuts that had already happened:

> *If we had allowed our spending* [since 1985–86] *to grow at the same rate as inflation and population change, our program expenditure this year would have been about $14.3 billion. Our budget for 1991–92 is only $11.5 billion. This government's expenditure management has saved $2.8 billion in program spending...*[12]

In other words, in real per capita spending the Province had reduced programs by 2.8 billion 1991 dollars in six years. The next year the treasurer again noted how program spending had been restricted:

Since 1985–86 we have limited program spending growth to just 2.3 percent per year [not adjusting for inflation or population growth].... *We held program expenditure almost flat last year. It was only 0.4 percent above the 1990–91 level....*[13]

In the turmoil of the times, though, these messages were ignored by the media and the opposition, and lost on the public. But they could hardly have been missed by Klein: as well as having participated in cabinet decisions to make the cuts, he was sitting nearby in his legislature seat as the treasurer made these statements.[14]

5

THE KLEIN CUTS:

WHERE ALBERTANS

STAND NOW

'WHEN OUR NEW administration took over a year and a half ago...we saw uncontrolled spending,' claimed Premier Klein in June, 1994.[15] The Klein government has worked hard to rewrite history, portraying the Getty government as extravagant spenders who drove Alberta to the brink of financial ruin. Playing on the public's memories of Novatel, Gainers, Magcan, and other financial messes, the Klein government has convinced people that costs under Getty were climbing without restraint. If history is written by winners, then the loser in *this* history is Don Getty's government, not Laurence Decore and the Alberta Liberals.

'Out-of-control spending' is a chorus the premier cannot stop chanting, even while he discussed his government's reinvestment plans in December, 1996: 'We knew we had to get spending under control. We knew it was literally going through the roof.'[16] This claim is the heart of his regime.

Health care spending has come in for particular distortion. For example, in the Alberta Health '1993–94 Annual Report,' the Minister of Health, Shirley McClellan, wrote '...our health system was quickly becoming unaffordable.'

Or, in a story on the 'success' of cuts to health care in the *Edmonton Journal* in May, 1995,[17] a government Public Affairs Officer said, 'Up until 1993–94, health-care costs had been rising about 12 to 13 per cent each year for the last decade.' This quote was featured prominently, giving the impression that soaring costs had been tamed by the Klein government.

This is a straightforward misrepresentation of the facts. The spokesman greatly exaggerates, making it appear that the increases of the last decade were much larger than they actually were. The Department of Health's annual reports from that period even calculate the changes for the reader: 1984/85 saw a '...3.6% increase in per capita expenditures.' The next year it was 6.4%, and the following year it was 7.5%. All these rises were happening during times of substantial inflation, which they do not account for; accounting for inflation would reduce these percentages even further.

Even in late May, 1996, after losing the by-election in Redwater and after years of cutbacks, Klein still argued his government was '...trying to get the cost of health care under control.'[18] At that point, the cost of health care was probably not just the lowest in Canada, but the lowest in North America.[19]

In the fall of 1996, Shirley McClellan's successor as Minister of Health, Halvar Jonson, continued the myth that health costs in Alberta were, in his word, 'spiralling': 'If health spending had continued to increase at the rate that was under way...we would probably be spending $7.5 [billion] or $8 billion on health care.'[20] No information supporting this claim was reported.

● ● ●

The gap between the political posturing of the Klein government and the reality of Alberta's situation is widely documented: it shows up in the government's own internal research, in the province's public accounts, and in Statistics Canada data. It has also been analyzed in detail by economists such as Melville McMillan, Chair of the Economics Department at the University of Alberta, and Allan Warrack, a former Progressive Conservative cabinet minister in Alberta and a professor in the University of Alberta Faculty of Business.

According to their analyses, Alberta's level of support for public programs had already fallen 15% in the late 1980s and early 1990s, adjusting for population growth and inflation.[21] This placed Alberta below the Canadian average two years before the Klein government's cuts even began.

When the Klein government announced its plans for cuts, their target was for another 20%. But the government did not make any adjustment for population growth and inflation. This is such an obvious oversight it seems reasonable to assume it was a deliberate way to understate the impact of the reductions. Population growth and inflation magnify the effect of the cuts, because an ever larger number of people end up scrambling for fewer dollars, the value of which is reduced by inflation. Once these factors are calculated, the real effect of the cuts would have been just over 30%.[22] Fortunately, the Klein government has not fully implemented the final stages of some cutbacks.

The Klein government's cuts did not begin in earnest until after the general election in June, 1993. The targets set for ultimate reductions ranged from 12% in Education to 47% in Municipal Affairs. In the first year, they cut more than $800 million from public spending. Public sector job reductions were immense, including in the first year alone 778 teachers and 2300 hospital staff. They reduced or eliminated various benefits and programs, usually with sharpest effect on seniors, families with young children, and the poor (though some benefits were actually increased to very low-income seniors). They imposed a five percent pay cut on MLAs and public-sector workers, including civil servants, teachers, nurses, and university staff. They raised health care insurance premiums substantially, while de-insuring many services.

The cuts continued the following year. By the end of 1995, public spending had fallen $1.9 billion since the Klein government came into office, and more than 4500 civil service jobs had been eliminated. Many hundreds more were cut in 1996. Direct fees and premiums for public services continued to climb. In Calgary the Grace Hospital, the Colonel Belcher Hospital, and the Holy Cross Hospital were closed, and the Calgary General/Bow Valley Centre was slated for closure. In Edmonton, where the Charles Camsell Hospital and General Hospital were already closing under previous plans, the Grey Nuns and

Misericordia were downgraded to 'community health centres,' and hospital-bed numbers were cut by 44% from 1994 to 1996.[23]

• • •

Under Ralph Klein's government, public programs in Alberta became the most poorly supported in Canada. The government's announced plans for reductions, if fully implemented, would have left Albertans far behind even the poorest Atlantic provinces: 15% less well supported than the lowest 'have-not' provinces and 20% to 25% less well supported than the other provinces that have balanced their budgets.[24] In the most controversial area, health care, Alberta's per capita spending in fiscal 1995/96 would have been 28% below the average of the other provinces with balanced budgets.

As it is, having implemented most of its plans, the government has wavered with some of the final cuts, reversed a few, and continued with others. The cuts occurred so quickly and in such confusion that they became hard to follow. By fiscal year 1995/96, per-student funding for schools dropped to 14% below the Canadian average.[25] From 1992 to 1995 the Calgary Regional Health Authority lost about 1400 staff, and the Capital Health Authority in Edmonton about 3000. From 1992 to 1995, the total province-wide loss of employed registered nurses was estimated at almost 8275, or a staggering 43% of all employed nurses in Alberta.[26] As these cuts continue, many jobs are being downgraded: during 1993 to 1997, according to announced plans, 30% of the nursing jobs at the University Hospital in Edmonton will have been eliminated or replaced by less-trained and lower-paid workers.[27]

Members of the boards of the regional health authorities are all appointed by the Klein government, and they seldom speak out. But occasionally they provide revealing information. The chairman of the finance committee of the Capital Health Authority in Edmonton, Bill Grace, was reported as saying, 'There has been a funding reduction in this region of $189 million in three years.... That is a reduction of 21.2 percent.'[28] It does not appear his figure accounts for either inflation or population growth, both of which would make the drop even larger.

The government's plans for 'reinvestment,' presented in the fall of 1996, do surprisingly little to improve this situation. For example, despite the hoopla around increased health care funding (including large newspaper advertisements from Alberta Health), only a small fraction of laid-off staff will be recovered; after eliminating 8275 nursing jobs, it appears that the government will support rehiring about 300 through its reinvestment.[29] While funding will climb during the 1996/97 election season, the planned increases for the two years after that will not keep up to inflation and population growth, and there will be, in effect, another round of cutbacks. One common reaction to the announcement of increased funding was to ask, 'Were the cuts necessary in the first place?' The answer is clear and raw: no.

• • •

Under the Getty government, support for Alberta's public programs went from the highest in Canada to below average; under the Klein government it hit bottom. This legacy is described succinctly in McMillan's study: 'Alberta is unique and anomalous as being the richest province...while providing the lowest level of provincial services in Canada.'[30]

While spending a lot does not guarantee good public services, spending too little does guarantee poor public services. The government did not ask the people of Alberta if they wanted support for public programs to reach the lowest levels in the country. Neither were Albertans informed that spending had been dropping for years before Ralph Klein became premier; in fact, the Progressive Conservatives under Klein repeatedly said the opposite. Annual deficits were large and the debt was growing, and the government claimed that public services were at fault.

It wasn't overspending on public programs that caused Alberta's debt to grow. Ordinary Albertans were blamed and punished for something they did not do.

6
THE LEAKY REPORT

THE SENIORS report we wrote for the Getty government and shredded for the Klein government was not the first report I saw accepted and prepared for public release, only to be concealed by political decision-makers. There is a basic tension in government between good policy and good politics. Whether from ideology or expediency, political leaders often commit to a position and then search for the evidence to support it. If evidence comes up they do not like, they sometimes ignore it, conceal it, or destroy it.

What was remarkable about this case was the scale of the deceit. There were the financial and human costs: almost one million dollars had been spent, and over a thousand people had been involved, some representing organizations involving thousands of others.

And there was the moral price: the public had participated with the understanding that results would be openly and honestly shared. When a promise of that kind is broken, people learn to distrust politics. Political leaders who get away with such ploys learn to ignore democracy.

I had never before considered leaking a document. It is accepted inside government that information needs to be handled with discretion, as it should be.

And while civil servants serve the public, they report to a government led by their political masters. The discipline of silence is imposed from the first day of work, when provincial employees must sign an oath of confidentiality. The threat of being fired for speaking out backs up this oath. It is also backed up by law, for 'The Public Service Act' imposes legal penalties on government employees who release information without authorization. In any case, leaking a document carries with it the sense of betraying your employer. It is a breach of trust.

I am not sure when I decided to leak the report. My decision occurred in stages. Even before we had shredded the report, the Premier was speaking about how costs in public programs were out of control. He was completely contradicting the best evidence I had seen, evidence from his own government. It looked as if the Klein government, using distorted information, was going to chop services to some of the very people who needed them and trusted government the most.

I paid to have photocopies of the report made at a private copy shop (more than a little ironic, given that I was helping to shred cartons of them). I told no one. As I pondered whether to send out the copies my imagination worked overtime. Would there be a widespread investigation? Would the police come to search my house?

These worries may sound a bit absurd. But remember, in a province where one party has utterly dominated political life for 25 years, the networks of power run wide and deep. I wasn't just risking legal

penalties and the end of my career in the civil service—the power of the government reaches into many
places I might some day want to work: companies
doing business with the government, for example, and
the universities. This was not a small risk.

If I knew then what I know now I would have
done things differently. I would have acted more
boldly. What I did was type an unsigned cover letter
and send the copies of the report to the opposition
parties and major newspapers. By this time, the team
that had worked on the report had been disbanded. I
had left the government to follow plans made long
before to study in Britain. It was May, 1993, and a
provincial election campaign was in full swing.

● ● ●

Bettie Hewes, running for the Liberals, used the
leaked document to charge that there had been a
cover-up. Ralph Klein denied the charge. Here is some
of the dialogue from the news coverage:

ON CTV:
*NEWSCASTER: ...Bettie Hewes released a document
that she said outlined major cuts in seniors' services
that were planned by the Conservatives. Tory leader
Ralph Klein, campaigning in Vegreville today,
reacted angrily to a charge that he'd covered up the
document. Klein said as well it really was just a discussion paper and he didn't cover up anything.*

*PREMIER KLEIN: What I find absolutely reprehensible
about this whole situation is that Mrs. Hewes said*

that I deliberately suppressed that document. Well
that is absolute, utter nonsense and I can say right
now, if that is what she said, boldly and plainly she
lied.

ON CBC TV:
PREMIER KLEIN: For Mrs. Hewes to call me to say that
I suppressed that report is an absolute, and I will
say this Bettie, a lie, an absolute lie. I had nothing to
do with that report whatsoever.

REPORTER: So will there be cuts to seniors...

PREMIER KLEIN: No. No. No. What we're saying is that
if there are any changes to seniors' programs it will
be done in consultation with the various represen-
tatives of seniors.

Was Ralph Klein telling the truth? The report was
suppressed by his government, but perhaps he didn't
know about it. Before becoming premier he had been
environment minister, so he would not have had
much connection to the report. On the other hand, it
was a major project of one of his cabinet colleagues, it
had been discussed at the cabinet table, and public
hearings on it had been held in his home town of
Calgary. And it was his government who ordered the
report destroyed.

One more detail: when I wrote the unsigned cover
letter to go with my leaked copies, I estimated the
cost of preparing the report at $700,000. It was an
educated guess that I deliberately kept low so as not

to exaggerate. In response to questions about this from the media, a member of the premier's staff compiled the costs. The result: the report cost more than $900,000. However, wanting to downplay the report, the premier's staff informed reporters that it cost about $250,000. Once again, the truth was dismissed as an inconvenience.

• • •

In August 1994 I returned from my year in Britain. I hoped the position of the Klein government had moderated from the election campaign and that their decisions would be more closely based on the best information. Instead, the Premier and his colleagues were continuing with the same misleading accounts, still telling people costs on public services were rising and needed to be cut.

So, not having kept a copy of the seniors report, I spent time reading Alberta's public accounts and Statistics Canada information, reconstructing similar information to what we had compiled for the seniors report, and collecting more. It was not hard: I already knew what to look for.

I began to write articles for the newspapers and speak to people about what the government was doing. In the winter of 1996, I was phoned by a group organizing citizens' hearings into the planned closure of the Calgary General Hospital. They had seen an article of mine in the *Calgary Herald* and wanted me to speak to their hearings. To prepare for my presentation, I dug up the most recent information I could, and it confirmed what I had seen three years earlier.

With the Klein government's cuts, Alberta's support for public services was now the lowest in Canada. Yet people were still being told more cuts were necessary.

As I drove home from my presentation about the shut-down of the Calgary General, I decided to try once again to get the truth out about the seniors report. I phoned the *Edmonton Journal* to give my account. The following Saturday their political columnist, Mark Lisac, ran the story.[31]

By Monday noon I had received no calls from the media, and no government lawyers had threatened legal action. I thought the story was over.

Then the wave hit: Monday afternoon two TV crews were at my house, and there were calls from radio stations, newspapers, and national news agencies. Throughout the week the story of the shredded report was covered in one form or another across the province. The government, obviously embarrassed, stumbled from denial to denial, changing stories and contradicting itself repeatedly.

At first, the government said it didn't know about the shredding and didn't have a copy of the report. Then the premier, referring to the report as 'ancient history,' claimed it was shredded '...for recycling purposes' and that 'there simply wasn't enough room to store the stuff.'[32] To embellish his story, the Premier said the report was too difficult for the public and seniors to read: 'It was so full of bureaucratese as to be almost unreadable.'[33] In fact, professional writers and editors had been hired to help prepare the report, and staff of the government's own Public Affairs Bureau edited it as well. Finally, to defuse a potentially explosive situation, the government released a copy of the report.

I received plenty of encouragement, and letters, cards, and even flowers. Of all these responses, one was the most telling. An employee of the government's Department of Health heard the story, closed the office door, looked up my phone number, and said, 'Thank you very much. The people of Alberta need to learn what is really happening.'

7

PRIVATE SECTOR SUBSIDIES IN FREE ENTERPRISE ALBERTA[34]

ONE OF THE great ironies of Alberta is that it claims to be a bastion of free enterprise, while in reality the Alberta government has spent more on subsidies to the private sector than any government in Canada.[35] Even today, despite claims that Alberta's government is 'out of the business of business,' private-sector subsidies remain at a generous level—this, while Alberta's support for most public programs is the lowest in the country.

From 1986 to 1995, the period when the Alberta government faced its toughest economic constraints, its spending on economic development (grants, tax breaks, loan guarantees, programs, and so on) exceeded $20 *billion*, a sum unrivalled by any other province. In fact, far more has been spent on this 'corporate welfare' than on income support for the poor. In fiscal 1994/95, for example, Alberta's expenditure on income support for the poor (or 'welfare,' as it is commonly called) totalled $608 million, less than half the amount spent on the category called 'industrial development.'[36]

The truth is, Alberta has had the most heavily subsidized private sector in Canada for 20 years. Yet the government has been unwilling to put the same pressure on these subsidies it has put on public programs. Subsidies are a big part of the political and economic system in Alberta, but they remain in shadows of secrecy. It is time to throw some light on them.

When the Conservatives first formed Alberta's government in 1971, provincial support for industrial development[37] was $64 million. This was a bit higher rate than other provinces, but not out of proportion to Alberta's wealth.

In 1972 and 1973, the Lougheed government revamped the petroleum royalty and marketing system in Alberta. In defiance of the angry energy industry, Lougheed removed the cap on royalties put in place by Social Credit. His timing was perfect, for in 1973 the price of oil leapt from $3 (US) a barrel to $17 (US) a barrel because of war in the Middle East. But this was the last time an Alberta government stood up forcefully to the private sector, placing public interest above private bank accounts.

In 1974 the scale of subsidies in Alberta began to change forever. Lougheed started speaking of the need to diversify Alberta's economy. In a speech to the Calgary Chamber of Commerce he said,

> *We perhaps have another decade left to diversify our economy, to become less dependent (as an aside we will always be of course extremely strong as a*

*resource province) but we must be in a position to be
less affected by external factors. If we fail to do so in
my view we will leave the next generation in Alberta
a sad legacy indeed—a lack of economic muscle to
sustain our quality of life over the longer term.*[38]

By the following year, 1975, spending on industrial
development had doubled from 1971, even after
adjusting for inflation and population growth. There
were various activities to cover, including the forma-
tion of the Alberta Energy Company, the creation of a
$100 million capital fund to establish the Alberta Oil
Sands Technology Re-search Authority, and the pur-
chase of Pacific Western Airlines. In 1975, the
Alberta government earned more in corporate taxes
($270 million) than it spent in industrial develop-
ment ($257 million). But virtually every year since
then, far more has been spent on industrial development than has been collected in corporate taxes.
Industrial development spending soared, reaching
heights the rest of Canada could simply gasp at.

By 1977 Alberta was spending in this area far
beyond the national average. Then in 1979 Lougheed
expanded the Tory commitment to economic diversification, set up a Department of Economic Development, and doubled this spending again. In 1981
industrial development expenditures were almost $1
billion. They continued soaring, and by 1983 more
was spent on industrial development than on social
services, transportation, environment, and culture
combined.

Still, it wasn't enough. In 1986, and again in 1987,
$3 billion was poured into this area, more than any

other area of spending except health care, which was marginally higher. In 1987 Alberta spent 11% above the national average on health care, and over 600% above average on industrial development. That was also when the Province began staggering into debt. In fact, in the six fiscal years from 1986/87 to 1991/92, when Alberta was running massive annual deficits, spending on industrial development exceeded the deficit in three of those years, and was close to the size of the deficit in the other three years.[39]

• • •

The flip side of these subsidies is the immense revenues the Alberta government receives from oil and gas sales.[40] These climbed sharply after the oil crisis in 1973. In 1971 they totalled $247 million, and at their peak in 1985 they reached $6 billion. In the past 25 years, the Alberta government has received almost twice as much in natural resource revenues as all the rest of Canada combined: a total of *$81 billion*. In the mid-1980s, Albertans were receiving through their provincial government more than 25 times the average of other Canadians in natural resource revenues.

Taking inflation into account, Alberta's oil and gas revenues since 1971 would be worth about $130 billion today. A hundred and thirty billion dollars would buy a new home at the current average price in Calgary for every household in Alberta. Or, it would put a millionaire in over half the families in greater Edmonton. The interest alone from this amount of money could finance most of the operations of the Government of Alberta.

This is very much like a lottery windfall. Albertans didn't put the oil and gas in the ground, it is just good fortune that we live on the territory above it. And like a lottery jackpot it is a one-time-only event: this money comes from a non-renewable resource, and when it is managed carelessly it is gone forever.

Unfortunately, virtually all this wealth *is* gone forever: the holdings of the Heritage Trust Fund[41] are a small fraction of this total, and even when the value of the Heritage Trust Fund is taken into account the Province has a net debt.

Alberta's unprecedented scale of private-sector subsidies—$34 billion in 25 years, not counting inflation—was made possible by this infusion of natural resource wealth. Alberta's petroleum resources are public wealth, a point often made by Peter Lougheed when he was premier. The effect of the policies of the Tory government has been a massive transfer of this public wealth into private hands, through subsidies. One cannot avoid asking: has this served most Albertans well in the long run?

The future is unlikely to be as generous to Albertans as the past 25 years have been. Conventional oil reserves are at less than half their peak, reached in the early 1980s. Industry estimates are that Alberta's conventional oil production will begin to drop off sharply after the year 2005, following the path of the original Leduc oilfield, which is now being wound down. Natural gas reserves will last longer, but they are also declining. The average size of gas pools found from 1980 to 1992 in Alberta is less than one-quarter the size of the pools found before 1980. The oil sands will last indefinitely, but they only produce a small portion of Alberta's petroleum royalties because of higher costs of production and lower royalty rates.[42]

•••

During Lougheed's years, petroleum revenues were so great the province enjoyed budget surpluses almost every year despite its huge expenditures on the private sector. In Don Getty's first year as premier, petroleum revenues plummeted and deficits jumped correspondingly. The provincial government, which was already providing large subsidies to stabilize the energy sector through uncertain times in the early 1980s, moved quickly to prop up the energy industry even more.

In each of April, June, October, and December of 1986, new subsidies were announced or existing programs increased. Among the biggest: the Royalty Tax Credit Program was made significantly more generous, the Alberta Petroleum Incentives Program was expanded, and the Exploratory Drilling Assistance Program was introduced. These, along with other energy sector subsidies, totalled $1.6 billion in fiscal 1986/87 alone. This is the operation of corporate welfare at its clearest.

As the petroleum sector and the economy as a whole recovered during the next several years, many subsidies began to decline. In fact, looking at his term as a whole, Getty did a decent job of cleaning up the expenditure problems in most areas of government, although this effort is little appreciated. Industrial development spending fell faster than most other programs, dropping from $3.1 billion in 1987 to about $2.1 billion in 1992.

As impressive as these cutbacks sound, they still left Alberta with unusually rich government spending to support private business: double the per capita rate of British Columbia, five times the rate of Ontario, and well over twice the national average. The $2.2 billion in industrial development spending in Alberta in 1992/93 compares to $2.7 billion on social services; $3.0 billion on education; $778 million on transportation and communications, $193 million on environment, and $208 million on recreation and culture.[43]

● ● ●

Here are two other ways of measuring the imbalance between private subsidies and public services:

1. In 1994/95, industrial development spending took almost twice the proportion of the provincial budget it did when the Progressive Conservatives first came to power. In 1971 it was 4.8% of the total provincial budget; in fiscal 1994/95 it was 9.4%.

2. Provincial government spending on industrial development was 24 times higher in 1994/95 than in 1971; all other provincial government

spending combined was about 12 times higher. (Neither figure adjusts for inflation or population growth.)

• • •

Alberta's private subsidies are even more startling when compared to the amount collected in corporate income taxes. From 1986/87 to 1992/93, all corporate income taxes paid to the Alberta government totalled $4.64 billion (not including taxes paid by family farmers).[44] The total cost of spending on industrial development (not including the $5.6 billion in agricultural subsidies) was $9.97 billion.[45] This means that in direct revenues and expenditures, *the corporate sector in Alberta was a net drain on the provincial taxpayer of $5.3 billion from 1986/87 to 1992/93*, the very period Alberta's debt increased so rapidly.

Under the Klein government, industrial development spending has continued to decline. With high oil prices, a booming economy, and a strong agricultural sector, the calls for subsidies have grown quieter. Even so, there have been significant tax reductions for business (for example, cuts to the Machinery and Equipment Tax paid by large businesses in rural areas, and to aviation and rail fuel taxes). More are scheduled to occur. Detailed information is not yet available, but preliminary figures would suggest that the booming corporate sector in Alberta is contributing less than two percent of total provincial expenditures, once subsidies are subtracted.[46] This would be less surprising in provinces with small corporate sectors, but Alberta is home to Canada's second-largest concentration of major corporations.

The 'Alberta Advantage' is clear: one should invest in Alberta but live elsewhere, benefiting from the low tax rates and high business subsidies here and enjoying the benefits of adequately funded public programs elsewhere. Alberta is becoming a tax resort for wealthy Canadians: 'Who needs the Cayman Islands when there is a tax haven right here in Canada,' a financial planner states in the newspaper.[47] Canadians can claim to be resident in Alberta for tax purposes while enjoying the advantages of living elsewhere. This is exactly the advice given in some circles. Giles Gherson, a national business columnist for Southam newspapers, quoted Larry Bell of Vancouver's Shato Holdings: 'Accountants are always telling you that if you put a subsidiary in Alberta, and you send executives there for so many days a year, they can pay lower taxes there rather than BC.'[48]

8

THE ALBERTA

ADVANTAGE

UP CLOSE

WHERE DO all the subsidies go? There are the infamous recipients that most Albertans will remember from news reports: Novatel, Magcan, Bovar, Gainers, and so on. As big as these were they only account for a small portion of the total. The really big bucks flow out the Treasury door in programs and tax breaks that few Albertans have heard of, programs supporting energy, tourism, and forestry, for example.

Using the provincial government's own accounts, Statistics Canada compiles industrial development spending into several major categories. The most recent period for which these details are available from Statistics Canada is 1986/87 to 1992/93, the time when Alberta's debt soared.

From 1987/88 to 1992/93, annual subsidies to agriculture grew significantly, almost doubling from just over $600 million to almost $1.2 billion.[49] In contrast, subsidies to oil and gas dropped from a high of over $1.6 billion in 1986/87 to $430 million in 1992/93.

Each of these sectors received $5.6 billion apiece during these years, together accounting for more than two-thirds of all such subsidies.

The other two large categories are Trade and Industry ($936 million) and Forestry ($806 million). These Statistics Canada figures do not include all forms of subsidy, such as the massive road and bridge projects built at public expense for the forestry industry, including $75 million in the Athabasca region for Alberta Pacific Forest Industries and $65 million for the Daishowa mill near Peace River. Nor do they include the value of loan guarantees, unless the guarantee is called by the bank. If these are included the value of subsidies to the forestry industry rises to $1.35 billion from 1987 to 1990 alone.[50]

One must ask whether these subsidies are about economic diversification, or about rewarding powerful interests. One of these powerful interests, the energy sector, will defend itself by saying it generates the royalties that make Alberta wealthy. But oil and gas are publicly owned resources, and royalties are a form of rent companies pay for the right to sell these resources. Oil and gas companies pay royalties much as a tenant pays rent to use a house (though at the end of the lease the landlord's house is still standing, while the oil and gas is gone forever). The tenant doesn't expect the landlord to pay for groceries in return for the rent. Why should the petroleum industry expect the public to pay their cost of doing business because they happen to pay royalties?

To put the scale of Alberta's subsidies to the energy sector in perspective, compare them to

Saskatchewan's. Alberta produces about 5 times as much petroleum as Saskatchewan does.[51] In total, the Alberta government earns roughly 8 times as much as Saskatchewan in petroleum revenues. In most years the Saskatchewan government spends between $10 million and $20 million to support this industry. In contrast, the Alberta government spent anywhere from $430 million to over $700 million on the energy industry from 1989 to 1993, and much more in the years before. For an industry that provides 8 times the revenue as Saskatchewan's, Alberta is providing 20 to 70 times the subsidies.[52]

• • •

THE LOST LOGIC OF SUBSIDIES

The appropriate logic behind taxpayer subsidies for private business is simple: the public should subsidize private industries because they generate public wealth. A strong private sector contributes to a strong public sector, paying taxes to support schools, roads, hospitals, and so on. In the language of Peter Lougheed, public support for the private sector helps build the 'economic muscle to sustain our quality of life over the longer term.'

In hindsight, the return on the Alberta taxpayer's investment in the private sector has been poor: for many years the Alberta government's spending on subsidies exceeded 500% the average of the other provinces, while spending on public services seldom exceeded 15% higher. Nonetheless, there was an argument to be made: if Albertans want fine schools and hospitals they should do whatever they can to attract tax-paying businesses.

The Klein cuts have reversed this logic. Albertans now receive the lowest public services in the country. It only stands to reason that Albertans should provide the lowest levels of subsidies to private business.

For example, it is time to question the hundreds of millions the Alberta taxpayer loses through the Royalty Tax Credit Program for the petroleum industry: $291 million in 1994/95 alone.[53] Similarly, the Department of Energy spent about $13 million in fiscal 1994/95 in direct support of research into the oil sands. Perhaps it is time to privatize this, or shut it down. If the private sector won't pay for it, why should taxpayers? Ending programs like these won't wipe-out Alberta's energy industry. Nor will it kill the golden goose of petroleum royalties. In Alberta's multi-billion-dollar oilpatch, these subsidies can be regarded as fat to be trimmed from the system.

The same could apply to the $11.7 million spent by the Department of Economic Development and Tourism on advanced technology projects, or any of the other programs supported by its $127 million budget in 1994/95. The Alberta government typically spends two to three times as much on tourism subsidies as the BC government, despite BC's larger population and huge tourism industry.[54]

• • •

It seems practically impossible to judge how much subsidy is the right amount. If $1 billion in subsidies is good, is $2 billion twice as good? On the other hand, perhaps they should be cut to $500 million, or even eliminated. It is risky to use taxpayers' money for such uncertain and unmeasurable results. The usual outcome seems to be that taxpayers pay a lot and get a little.

Subsidies in a relatively free market contradict the very economic principles that Progressive Conservatives claim to cherish. Market forces should, they say, be allowed to function unfettered when suppliers and consumers are relatively free. If drilling an oil well is not profitable at $18 a barrel, free-market economics argues that the taxpayer should not subsidize the industry to make it profitable. If a pulp mill requires government loan guarantees, free-market economics argue that the mill should not proceed.

History shows that subsidies are not a form of economic development so much as they are a form of corporate welfare. The evidence on this is clear: for the past 15 years subsidies have been highest when the economy is weakest, and lowest when the economy is strongest. It is the same pattern one finds in unemployment insurance and welfare programs. When times are tough the government is there to smooth the business cycle and stabilize the economy. Yet one would expect the opposite if subsidies were about economic development: when a lot is being spent, as it was during 1985 to 1989, the economy should flourish. It hasn't worked that way.

Business subsidies of the kind typical in Alberta should be known for what they are—welfare—and judged and managed accordingly. If low public benefits are good medicine in the harsh world of individual poverty, they should also be good medicine in the business world. Or, if generous government support helps businesses flourish and grow, generous support in the form of education, health, and social

benefits will do the same for individuals. It is hypo-
critical and unfair to apply a double standard to the
benefit of select Albertans.

● ● ●

Subsidies to the private sector are now built into the
basic structure of Alberta's economy and politics;
they are taken for granted and never questioned.
What political leader is willing to vigorously argue
that it is time to put industrial development spending under the microscope of public scrutiny?

Industrial subsidies go beyond positions of left-
wing or right-wing economics. People on all parts of
the political spectrum should challenge this distortion of the free market, and this warping of public
policy. While the Klein government might reject
these criticisms by calling them 'socialist,' they are in
fact pointing to a problem in basic fairness: welfare
for corporations, the law of the jungle for ordinary
citizens.

It is time to ask a few questions:

1. If government spending on public programs is
   so low, why should government spending to
   subsidize the costs of certain industries be
   high?
2. Is all the fat trimmed out of these subsidies? If
   not, why not?
3. Is it the role of the ordinary taxpayer to cover
   the costs of public services *and* to underwrite
   the operating costs of major industries?

4. Do small entrepreneurs in Alberta, struggling to pay taxes, realize they are supporting some of the biggest and most powerful businesses in the province?

5. Why doesn't the Alberta government tabulate all its spending on industrial development and private sector subsidies into a single annual report, in the same manner that all spending on health, education, the environment, and other areas is presented in annual reports?

6. Given that Alberta has the lowest tax rate in Canada, why do some industries need such big subsidies?

7. If the economy flourished in 1971 when subsidies were under five percent of the province's budget, why do they need to be double that level now?

• • •

Does this feel like an attack on sacred cows? While there is a justification (strong or weak) for each of these subsidies, there are also justifications for adequate hospitals, schools, environmental safeguards, and so on. Low public services should correspond to low private subsidies.

Alberta's established pattern of corporate welfare could break down during the next down-turn in Alberta's economy. Alberta has the most volatile economy in Canada, swinging from spectacular highs to sharp lows. During the lean years of the 1980s, as we have seen, taxpayers provided billions of dollars in relief to the energy and agriculture sectors, as well as accepting marked cuts to public programs. In the next downturn, public programs will already be at low levels, so the public may not tolerate another round of massive corporate welfare along with further cuts to public programs.

• • •

When it set out to cut health, education, and other public-program spending, the Klein government set arbitrary targets, prohibited input from anyone directly involved in those sectors, published the names and salaries of top public executives, and ignored or bullied any opposition. Here is a proposal to get the out-of-line costs of industrial development spending under control, using similar techniques:

STAGE ONE: Appoint a commission to review and report on industrial-development spending. The commission would include a health-care economist, a doctor, a nurse, a teacher, senior citizens, a small-business operator, a labour leader, a minimum-wage employee, and other ordinary Albertans. No representatives of industries benefiting from subsidies could serve on the commission.

STAGE TWO: Hold a series of 'Roundtable Meetings' to discuss the findings of this commission and stir public debate. Hand-pick each participant and carefully orchestrate the proceedings to insure the desired outcome.

STAGE THREE: Pass legislation to force cuts in private-sector subsidies to the same below average levels as other government spending. Establish a committee to oversee the cuts, explicitly excluding anyone from industries benefiting from the cuts from the committee. Appoint a cabinet minister to compile and track all subsidies and make the findings public.

STAGE FOUR: Publish regular progress reports on the declining subsidies, including any payments exceeding $100,000 (complete with corporate names and exact amounts). Dismiss all objections as whining.

9

PULLING

THE WOOL

AS OF LATE 1996, most Albertans were convinced that the costs of public programs were high and rising when Ralph Klein became premier, and that his government was 'out of the business of business.' As we have seen, both of these beliefs are false. A government doesn't pull the wool over citizens' eyes like this without some skillful technique.

With this government—and every government— citizens are well advised to recognize some of the tricks of the political trade. In societies run by emperors and generals, political power must be displayed: the sight of fortresses and soldiers intimidates people, and the pomp of royal tours and military parades strikes awe and demands submission. In modern democratic societies, where citizens are educated and expect their voices to be heard, power must be concealed. It must work quietly and unnoticed to shape what people 'know,' what they ignore, what they value, and how they think. Power may even deny its own existence: 'I am not powerful; I only do what you want.' The Klein government understands modern power.

• • •

THE SMOKESCREEN

A month after becoming Premier, Ralph Klein spoke to the Edmonton Downtown Rotary Club about his government's financial problems:

> ...the problem is spending; and the cause of that spending is a public that expects and demands more government than is needed.... Fully 83% of our revenues go to four areas: health, education, social services, and debt servicing. If those four areas were to go unchecked in the future as they have in the past, with a flat revenue scenario, by 1998 those four areas would consume 100% of our budget. There would be no money to pave roads, to protect the environment, to run our court system....

It was the kind of statement he made many times.

Strictly speaking he may have been telling the truth. But at the same time he was seriously misleading his audience. He was using the 'smokescreen,' in which *some* information is used to screen and distort other information. Of the four areas Klein mentioned, costs in three of them—health, education, and social services—had been stable or declining for about six years. Only debt servicing was rising, a result of massive business subsidies, high interest rates, and declining petroleum revenues. Debt servicing costs were the smokescreen the government used to conceal the drop in public-program spending.

His audience, understandably, was convinced by his statement that the costs of health, education and social services were out of control and would soon devastate the operation of the entire government, leading to everything from bad roads and pollution to a broken-down justice system. They may even have accepted that the fault was theirs for demanding more government than is needed. The statement was a superb piece of propaganda.

The smokescreen continues to be a favourite technique for this government whenever it needs to obscure the truth. Another example came in June, 1996, when newspapers reported that the government had announced its level of spending was only about five percent below the Canadian average. Averages are a smokescreen for details. If my sister married Wayne Gretzky, every member of my family would be a millionaire—on average. In reality only Wayne (and my lucky sister) would be. Similarly, while the rate of government spending in Alberta may be 5% below the other provinces *on average*, in many areas it is 15% to 20%—or more—below other provinces, while industrial development spending remains far *higher* than in other provinces.

● ● ●

THE FAKE

The fake is the simplest, bluntest, and perhaps the riskiest public relations manœuvre. It simply involves saying something that isn't true, often using information taken out of context. Most people call it lying. To be successful, it must be done with confidence and gusto. The bigger the better, because the public is more inclined to suspect someone will mislead them on a detail than on something really big. It is essential to the success of the fake that no one in a prominent position (such as the media) check on its facts. Here are some examples.

In March, 1994, the Minister of Health, Shirley McClellan, responded to an *Edmonton Journal* editorial that criticized cutbacks in health care by writing a letter to the editor:

> *[W]e can no longer measure the health of a society by counting up the number of hospital beds, MRI units, nurses per shift, and drugstores per square hectare. This type of health system accounting has contributed to health costs doubling in Alberta in the last 12 years....*

She provided no evidence to support her claim that health costs had doubled in 12 years, with good reason: by any *reliable* measure they had not. But this 'doubling' was stated as bold fact by a minister of the government and printed unchallenged by a major newspaper, so readers can be expected to believe it.

Even when specific numbers *are* presented, they are no guarantee of truthfulness. Here is a particularly clever example made by the premier himself in April, 1996, in a speech to the annual meeting of the Association of Canadian Medical Colleges, in Edmonton:

> *In the 1980s, health costs in this province tripled. The rate of growth exceeded the rate of inflation, which was roughly 40 percent over that decade. Meanwhile, the population grew by only 10 percent.... Not only were real costs rising, but health was consuming a growing proportion of our spend-*

ing. In Alberta, the figure jumped from 20 percent of the provincial budget in 1982, to 30 percent in 1992.

This is a carefully worded passage, giving listeners the impression he accounts for inflation and population growth. But if you read it carefully he never actually says 'per capita spending tripled after accounting for inflation,' he just leaves you thinking he does.

In the text of the speech the word 'tripled' is underlined. Obviously the Premier didn't check Shirley McClellan's letter above, where she said health costs had only doubled. In any case here is a quick check of the facts. The Alberta government's spending on health in 1980/81 was $1.6 billion; in 1989/90 it was $3.5 billion, a bit more than double.[55] But as the government's own graph on page 18 shows, when one accounts for inflation and population growth, health spending grew about 45% in the first four years of the 1980s, and changed little the rest of the decade. And for the record, in 1982 health costs were 23% of total spending; in 1992 they were 24%. Since 1970 they have almost always stayed in the range of 21% to 25% of total spending. They did not triple during the 1980s. They did not double. They did not jump from 20% to 30% of total provincial spending.

● ● ●

THE HOUDINI

With the Houdini, things mysteriously disappear. Things like billions of dollars in private-sector subsidies. Without a well-executed Houdini, Albertans might have demanded that industrial development spending be reined in. But you can't rein in what you can't see.

The Houdini can get complicated, but it all comes down to one thing: managing appearances. The secret to a magic trick is to get the audience to concentrate so hard on what you want them to see they don't notice any manipulation, even if it is happening right under their noses. The same principle works in politics.

In Alberta it is easy to notice spending on health, education, social services, transportation, and the environment. Each of these has its own department with its own budget and its own cabinet minister. These departments are frequently in the news, and every year they publish annual reports.

But have you ever heard of a 'Minister of Private Sector Subsidies'? Never. Could you easily find out the government's budget for subsidies? No, because there is no such thing.

While everyone's attention can be easily drawn to the latest budgets for the Departments of Health or Education, spending on industrial development is broken up among several departments and is tabulated in many forms. Part of it is in Treasury, part in Energy, part in Agriculture, and so on. It is tough to follow, and the government is not interested in making it easier.

So the stage is well set for the Houdini, and the rest is up to the performers in the Klein government. They guide the audience's attention to the centre of their spotlight: 'Look over here! The problem is spending on hospitals and schools and seniors.' They tell the audience there is nothing else to see: 'We are out of the business of business!' And so the magic of the Houdini plays itself out.

There can be clues that you are being fooled by the Houdini. For example, if a chart has a big category labelled 'Other,' beware. Everything you are not supposed to see could be hiding there. Here is a good illustration:

Expenditures	*1991–92*
Health	$3.352 billion
Education	$2.570 billion
Family and Social Services	$1.500 billion
Debt Servicing Costs	$1.136 billion
Other	$4.606 billion

This table is from the report of the Alberta Financial Review Commission, which was appointed by Treasurer Jim Dinning in January, 1993. They were 'prominent business executives and financial experts' who were given two months to make recommendations and help 'clearly communicate the province's financial situation to its citizens.' Their work was used to stir up public concern about government spending.

What's the biggest category in this table? 'Other.' So many things have disappeared into this category it dwarfs even health care. But what becomes the focus of all the public worry? Health, education, social services, and debt servicing costs. Subsidies to the private sector, among other things, are invisible.

• • •

RUBBER YARDSTICKS

A yardstick is great for measuring things because it's always 36 inches long. A person can count on the fact that a yard is a yard is a yard. Unless, that is, the yardstick is made of rubber. Then it can be stretched or squeezed to suit the circumstances. It's not much good for measuring things, but it sure can fool people.

We use one of the greatest of rubber yardsticks everyday: money. A dollar is a dollar, except that a dollar was worth a lot more 15 years ago than today. And there we have one of the Klein government's favourite rubber yardsticks. By ignoring inflation the cost of government services can be made to look like it has grown rapidly in the last decade, when really it hasn't. The same thing is true for population growth. Of course costs are going to rise if we have a bigger population, and generally that's no problem because revenues do too. Obscuring these facts are the most common ways this government has created the illusion that health costs soared out of control in the years before Klein became premier.

The 'reinvestment' plans to increase health care funding announced by the Klein government in the fall of 1996 are another great example of rubber yardsticks. According to government figures, by 1999 funding will have returned to almost the level of 1992. But if inflation runs at 2% per year and population growth at 1.5% per year, real per capita spending in 1999 will still be roughly 27% lower than in 1992.

So *be very careful* with government statements on costs if they do not say in big bold letters they account for both inflation and population growth. If you aren't, you could become the victim of the rubber yardstick.

Rubber yardsticks get sneakier than just ignoring inflation and population growth. For example, the government has often justified its claim that health costs were climbing by comparing them to other programs, such as education, environment and transportation. In this case, the rubber yardsticks are these other programs. Here is how it works: if some programs are smaller now than they were years ago, it can make programs that are not smaller appear to be growing in comparison, even if they aren't. If health costs have fallen 10% but are compared to other costs that have fallen 20%, it can easily appear that health costs have actually increased, but they haven't—they're just not shrinking as fast.

The Premier himself gave an excellent example of this kind of rubber yardstick in November, 1996. Speaking about 'reinvestment,' he said, 'Had we kept on the same course, health costs by the year 2000 would represent half the [total provincial] budget.'[56] By comparing health to the rest of the budget, which itself had been cut sharply, he made health costs appear to be climbing.

● ● ●

There are other tricks to watch for. For example, repetition. If you tell people something often enough ('We've got a spending problem....we've got a spending problem....we've got a spending problem....') they will start to believe you. A good slogan told a thousand times is invaluable. Have you noticed how many slogans there are around the Klein government? 'The Alberta Advantage.' 'We're out of the business of business.' 'We've got a spending problem, not a revenue problem''He listens, he cares.' If it sounds like a marketing campaign, that's because it is, and you are its target.

In the right circumstances it is surprisingly easy to mislead a lot of people. People love simple answers to difficult political problems, and are often more convinced by the simple answer than the correct one. The Klein government has offered people a simple answer to the problem of public debt and deficits. The government has succeeded in convincing people it is telling the truth. With the help of a handful of communications techniques, Ralph Klein and his spin doctors have had their way.

Two centuries ago the French social reformer, J.M. Servan, described how power is most effectively commanded. Ideas, said Servan, must be strongly linked, and must

> ...follow one another without interruption.... When you have thus formed the chain of ideas in the heads of your citizens, you will be able to pride yourselves on guiding them and being their masters. A stupid despot may constrain his slaves with iron chains; but a true politician binds them even more strongly by the chain of their own ideas; it is at the stable point of reason that he secures the end of the chain; this link is all the stronger in that we do not know of what it is made and we believe it to be our own work....[57]

In Alberta, the chain seems complete, and its links appear so reasonable and clear: out-of-control spending on public programs, a burgeoning debt, special interest groups whining when they don't get their way, a public that expects too much and pays too little. And we are told the ideas for the government's actions are our own: 'Most of all, you told us to get our financial house in order,' Premier Klein told an audience in Fort Macleod, speaking as he so often has. 'So we got down to work. You asked me to do it. We're doing it.' The audience rose to its feet and gave a roaring ovation.[58]

10
THE SPIN

DOCTORS

LIKE A GOOD advertisement, Ralph Klein can create an image of authority without providing authoritative information. He can sound credible without telling the whole truth. Like commercials that tug at heart-strings and make a person feel good but provide no solid information, Klein can create good feelings without much concern for the underlying substance. This is not unique to the Klein government. What is unusual is the remarkable skill with which they have done it.

Ralph Klein, a veteran television reporter, is so smooth one must conclude that even when he fumbles, he's being as deliberate as a broadcaster pretending to choose his words spontaneously when really he's reading them from a prepared text. His political technique is so good he no longer needs sincerity. But Klein has not pulled off his tricks alone.

Central to the success of the Klein government is an agency called the Public Affairs Bureau. It is the home of the government's media and public relations specialists, the 'spin doctors.' The Public Affairs Bureau is little known to Albertans, but is an important vehicle for carrying off the Klein government's agenda. It was created in the 1970s to coordinate government communications, ironically to make them more professional and less prone to purely political manœuvres. It produced a wide range of public information (such as brochures) and was also given functions such as administering the government logo and managing the Queen's Printer. The Bureau was usually assigned to a cabinet minister as a secondary responsibility.

The political importance of the Public Affairs Bureau gradually increased as it took a greater role in managing government relations with the media. Then, as funding reductions in recent years choked off the public information role of the Bureau, the shift from public service to political service intensified.

To understand the shadowy power of the Public Affairs Bureau one must first understand how government departments are organized. The head of every department (Health, Education, Community Development, and so on) is a cabinet minister, an elected government MLA who is appointed to cabinet by the premier. She or he is responsible, with other cabinet ministers and government MLAs, for making the broad decisions that set the directions for government policies and programs. Cabinet ministers are traditionally accountable for all activities of their departments.

Reporting to every cabinet minister is a deputy minister, who is responsible for implementing the decisions of the elected politicians and for running the day-to-day business of the department. Deputy ministers must work closely with cabinet ministers.

They are considered the top bureaucrat rather than a junior political figure, though in practice they must move skillfully in both worlds. Usually they stay with a department much longer than any particular cabinet minister, and traditionally they were experts in the department's particular area of responsibility. Every employee of a department reports ultimately to the deputy minister.

The Public Affairs Bureau is different. Select members of its staff occupy special positions in government. These people—holding the positions of 'Director of Communications,' or the less-senior 'Public Affairs Officer'—are trained and experienced specialists in public relations, the media, and political marketing. In other times they would be called 'propagandists.'

These people are assigned to be members of the senior management teams of all major government departments. At the political level, each works intimately with the cabinet minister assigned to each department. But they also participate in the top administrative meetings of departments. They commonly have offices near the deputy ministers. However, their first line of accountability is not to the deputy ministers running those departments; they report through their own separate channels, independent of normal government departments.

And this is where Klein made a little-noticed but important move when he became premier. Instead of assigning the Public Affairs Bureau to a cabinet minister as a secondary responsibility, he put himself in charge. With this stroke he became head of a network that reached throughout the civil service, but was parallel to it. This increased the ability of his office to control the government and influence the media and the public. While the Public Affairs Bureau retains its own managing director, in practice it is run from the Premier's Office.

This provides the Premier's Office with a direct and widespread means of surveillance throughout the bureaucracy, a kind of Big Brother presence. Directors of Communications often work from 'secure telephones' so their conversations cannot be easily intercepted. They meet together as a group weekly. They can quickly identify trouble spots, threatening issues, and personnel who may not suit the government's political needs. They also influence policy, layering political concerns over top of policy issues. This reduces the impartiality of the civil service and makes it more politically partisan, for everyone with whom Public Affairs staff work knows the special place they occupy.

This influence is made more intense, as one insider told me, because of pressure on staff of the Public Affairs Bureau to join the Progressive Conservative party. While being told that Tory membership isn't mandatory, they are also reminded that 'GM workers do not drive Toyotas to work.' Some Public Affairs Bureau staff have become closely tied personally to cabinet ministers, and they move with them when the ministers are shuffled to new posts.

These same officers are the primary spokespersons for each department to the media and the public. For example, when the public hears someone speaking through the media as a spokesman for the

Department of Health, usually the person they hear works for the Public Affairs Bureau and reports through it to the Premier's Office, speaking *as if* he or she worked for the Department of Health.

This approach elevates image over substance, because the spokespersons are specialists in public relations, not in the policies and programs of the departments to which they are assigned. They provide a centralized means for managing the political impact of all government communications to the public. Press releases, reports, and sensitive letters are reviewed, edited and approved for release by the Public Affairs Bureau before being made public. For example, if the Public Affairs Bureau feels an item concerning the environment, health, or social services may cause political problems it can, in effect, over-rule department experts, changing or even cancelling the material.

• • •

The mandate of the Public Affairs Bureau is written in its business plan:[59] 'The Public Affairs Bureau supports the government in its ongoing dialogue with Albertans by providing quality communications services and consulting.' The first core function listed for the Bureau is this: 'coordinating cross-government communications, including seconding communications professionals to government departments to coordinate, plan and implement government communications programs.'

Translated into plain English, this means it is vitally important that the Public Affairs Bureau assign its staff to every government department to insure all departments are singing from the same political songbook. The Public Affairs Bureau 'coordinates, plans, and implements' what all the departments say to the public.

In effect, the Public Affairs Bureau is now the Progressive Conservative party's marketing department. Paid for by the taxpayer, its function is to sell the Progressive Conservative government to the voter. Its staff defend, deflect, and deny criticism. They work to gain sympathetic coverage from the media. They counsel cabinet ministers and department staff about what is politically acceptable to say, and they offer training programs for government MLAs and senior bureaucrats to smooth out their dealings with the public and media.

The value the Premier places on his communications staff is indicated by their salaries. While other provincial employees and even MLAs have faced pay-cuts and layoffs, the salaries of the top communications staff have climbed. The premier's director of communications, reports the *Edmonton Journal*, has had substantial raises each of the past two years. He now earns $98,000 in salary and benefits and is provided with a government car.[60]

In the private sector in recent decades there has been a 'marketing revolution.' Marketing has gone from once being one area among several—finance, production, research, distribution—to being the dominant function of many corporations. The number one purpose of business, says management guru Peter Drucker, is to create customers.[61] Companies are advised to consider the needs of marketing in every area, from product research to staff training. Nothing should be done without its effect on marketing being considered.

This approach has rubbed off on government, where the main task has become 'political marketing.' No policy is endorsed, no statement made to the media, no letter from the public answered, and no report issued without its impact on political marketing being carefully weighed. If government claims cannot be legitimately supported, they may be illegitimately justified. If it doesn't help create a 'political customer'—that is, a loyal voter—it isn't likely to get far. In the process, well-informed debate inside government is sacrificed. Questions such as, 'Is it *right* that we do this? Is this *fair*? Are we telling the *truth*?' are seldom considered.

Politics always has this element, but in Alberta's government today it has become the main element, overshadowing all others. Under the Klein government the Public Affairs Bureau now has the organizational preeminence to stamp every major office of the government into a political form loyal not to the voter, or the person needing service, or the principles of democratic government, but to the Tories.

11

THE PARABLE OF

'AL AND BERTA':

TELLING STORIES

IN POLITICS

EVERYONE LEARNS stories, and everyone tells stories. We teach our children lessons about life with stories: stories of the little boy who cried wolf, or of children rewarded by Santa for behaving well. We share our lives and make friends by telling stories about what we did on the weekend, or about how our job is going. Religions teach their lessons through stories. Virtually every item on a newscast is presented as a story.

Politicians are among the most important story-tellers in society today. If members of the public are told a convincing story they will do remarkable things. Entire societies can be moved to great or terrible achievements by stories, building pyramids to deliver their kings to the underworld, setting up death camps to exterminate undesirable people, or rallying to overthrow a dictator. Today's politicians, like leaders throughout history, understand and take advantage of this.

A lot of psychological research now shows that we learn much more than we realize through stories.[62] They help us make sense of our world. It is hard to appreciate that stories are so important, because we have been taught since grade one that the important things to know are facts and theories. But much of the time what we really do is arrange what we experience to suit stories we already know. In other words, we make the facts fit the story, not the other way around.

So it is important to check every story against reality. For example, before 1492 most people accepted the story that the world is flat, and that sailors who went too close to the edge would fall off or be eaten by sea monsters. Then Columbus sailed towards the edge and, instead of falling off, he bumped into the Americas. Pretty quickly the old story of a flat Earth was dropped; it didn't stand up to the evidence.

Ralph Klein is an outstanding communicator, which means he is a master storyteller. He and his Public Affairs Officers know how powerful a good story is. A favourite story of theirs has been about the family who lived the high life, only to discover it was living beyond its means and heading for a financial mess. This, they say, is just like what was happening to Albertans until this government rode to the rescue.

In fact, the government even invented a family to stand in for all Albertans. 'Our story begins with an Alberta dream family of thirty years ago,' starts 'The Story of Al and Berta.' The story was published in the glossy workbook *Right on the Money*, prepared under

Provincial Treasurer Jim Dinning for the much-vaunted 'Budget Roundtable on the Debt and Deficit' held in March, 1993. This was part of the lead-up to the provincial election won by Klein's Tories. 'They were the perfect couple,' the story continues,

> *well groomed, happily employed, living the good life. They raised children, took holidays and bought things they wanted....*
>
> *Look at them now—living in a large rambling house, with a two car garage, safely in the suburbs. Al works as an executive in the oil business, Berta is also a professional. They have two kids, Bonnie and Kevin, both finishing school and ready to imitate Mom and Dad, and lead the good life....*
>
> *One day, Al's life is changed when his company faces bankruptcy and he's forced to take a major cut in pay in order to keep his job. Berta still has a job but there isn't as much security as there once was and she worries she may lose her job....*
>
> *How can they go from being successful people with a comfortable lifestyle, to a family struggling to make just the minimum payment each month on the credit cards, let alone retire the principal? Like their city, their province, and their country, Al and Berta face a mounting debt and a new reality, and it isn't pretty....*
>
> *The story of Al and Berta is not much different from the story of Alberta....*

The story ends in suspense. What will happen to Al and Berta? There is a pencil drawing of them beside the story, looking perfect and well-groomed. The story continued more than a year later, in *Beyond the Bottom Line*, the workbook for another budget round-table organized under Jim Dinning in September, 1994.

> *It's been almost 18 months since we first met Al and Berta.... Theirs was a dream life that turned to a nightmare of debt, mounting bills, and worries for their future and their children's. It's a story that closely parallels the financial plight of Alberta....*
>
> *They faced new realities, tough choices, a burden of financial commitments and expectations that exceeded their pocketbook....*
>
> *So what's happened since then? Big changes, and not all happy ones. On the financial side, things are looking better. After hours of agonizing debates, Al and Berta finally decided to sell their big house in the suburbs. It was a painful decision....*

After detailing Berta's job loss and her start-up of a small business, and describing the hard decisions they made about living within their means, the 'Story of Al and Berta' ends with cautious optimism: chastened by living in a house in the suburbs and helping their children go to college, Al the oil executive (who never did lose his job) and Berta the professional are living in a 'modest, reasonably-priced condominium' and nervously weighing their options for the future.

This story, of course, is bare-faced propaganda. But it works. The stories of Al and Berta began both of the workbooks that were given to the carefully selected participants in the roundtables. The stories set up the carefully chosen facts that followed in the rest of the documents, and because the stories and facts fit together so well the conclusions of the round-tables were virtually predetermined.

The story of the spendthrift family is a favourite of the Klein government, turning up frequently in speeches and comments. In January, 1994, Ralph Klein gave a province-wide television address to Albertans on the need for cutting public services. Near the beginning of his speech he told this story:

> *Imagine a family that spends more than it earns year after year. For every dollar they earn, they spend $1.20, so they end up borrowing 20% more than they earn. They put that extra 20% on their credit cards. In the meantime, the bills keep coming in.... Before long, this family has run up their credit cards to the maximum just to pay for their extra spending....*
>
> *Imagine this family so deep in debt, that they borrow even more money just to pay the interest on what they owe.*
>
> *Month after month, the bills arrive, the credit card invoices pile up, and still the family spends. Well, if they can't stop themselves, someone else will, and eventually they just won't be able to get credit.*
>
> *This is exactly where we were headed as a province....*

Klein and other members of his government have used the family metaphor repeatedly, speaking of the need to do renovations and the mess these involve, or of the need to get our 'financial house in order.' And they have tailored the facts to fit the story.

Once Albertans had come to accept these stories of the spendthrift family, it was easy to convince them that cutbacks to public services were not just a necessary evil, but good medicine. The problem is, the stories do not fit the evidence.

But no matter.

In propaganda the important consideration is not whether information accurately describes an objective situation but whether it *sounds* true. Facts are routinely taken out of context and misused to provide a misleading picture of the whole.[63]

Spending on hospitals, schools and seniors was not out of control when Ralph Klein became premier, any more than a piece of the sky fell on Chicken Little's head.

• • •

The story of the boy who cried wolf teaches about not asking for help unnecessarily. The stories about the spendthrift family from the Klein government teach Albertans that government cutbacks are the fault of ordinary Albertans. It was average Albertans who made the decisions that led to Alberta's financial problems. It was overspending on public services to meet the unreasonable claims of the public that nearly bankrupted the province. At a stroke, the Tory government absolves itself of all blame.

What the Klein government's stories do is explain problems, lay blame, and provide solutions. For the government they fulfill the maxim: 'Explain away what you can't forget, and forget what you can't explain away.' Just as Al and Berta were at fault for their financial woes, the government wants the voter to feel at fault for Alberta's financial woes. It is as if Progressive Conservative government decisions and policies never existed. This works so well because stories do not just help explain things away, they help people to remember some things and forget others. Stories provide a basis for selecting memories.

In politics the first contest is for the voter's memory, the second for her or his assent. If a politician can win the first he or she is more than halfway to winning the second. The trick is to tell a convincing story that voters can easily repeat to themselves— even better, to someone else. In politics, as in a court of law, the truth is not absolute. The truth is whatever story people can be persuaded to believe, whether they are judge, jury, or voter.

● ● ●

A story that better fits the evidence would be this one I have written:

> *Al and Berta are hard-working parents, happily married with two young children. Every week-day morning is a hurry as they get ready for work and help their children with breakfast and last-minute arrangements for playtime. Al and Berta then rush to their jobs, where they give their best. Al and Berta grew up in families that had known some lean times, when providing the basics of food and shelter was all that could be managed, even with hard work. Things are better now, but they still watch*

their finances carefully to cover all the expenses of a family.

Then one day the impossible happens. Berta inherits a fortune in oil and gas rights from a distant uncle. Overnight Al and Berta are multi-millionaires!

The next several months are a blur of excitement and complicated decisions. Al and Berta pay off their mortgage and car loan, and take a holiday to mull things over. This is a lot of money, and properly managed it will set up Al and Berta and their children for life. Pretty quickly they decide they need help managing it properly: choosing investments, minimizing taxes, establishing trust funds for the children, revising wills, and so on. And both Al and Berta decide to keep their jobs, because they enjoy them and believe hard work is important.

Al and Berta carefully select a firm of financial advisers that seems to offer everything. The members of the firm are trustworthy, conservative, hard-working, pleasant, and well-trained. With their help the inheritance seems to work magic. Al and Berta live like never before, buying a new house and car and going on holidays around the globe. And despite spending so much money, Al and Berta seem to keep getting richer. They set up a trust for their children to help them through whatever rainy days the future may hold. It is easy for them to forget that it all started with a lucky break; now it seems like their money is a natural right.

As time passes Al's and Berta's affairs become so complicated with corporate buy-outs and massive business deals that they let their financial management team take over the full operation of their fortune. With their jobs and family, Al and Berta just don't have time to keep up with all the demands and still become experts in financial management. As the years pass, Al and Berta renew their financial manager's contract for a second time, and then a third.

After ten years of this upward spiral, though, things suddenly flatten out, and even slip a little. Al and Berta's advisers assure them things aren't too bad, that this sort of thing was inevitable and precautions have been taken. Al and Berta agree to cut back on some of their expenditures, and although many members of the original financial team have now changed they renew the contract again. It is hard to imagine life without them.

But times do not improve. Each year Al and Berta take another cut, and despite this the value of their fortune keeps getting smaller. Meetings with their advisers become a bit more difficult. The firm promises the decline will end.

But then Al and Berta start to worry, because they notice a lot of money is being borrowed to compensate for the drop in income from their fortune. When they question the advisers they are assured it is not a problem, and that next year income will rise again and there won't be a need to borrow any more. The advisers stop adding to the trust fund for the children, and sell some of Al and Berta's favourite assets. After six years of steady cuts life isn't nearly as easy as it once was.

Just before renewing the advisers' contract for the seventh time, several members of the team *change. Al and Berta meet with them and level some tough questions. They come back with tough answers: things really are pretty bad because, after all, Al and Berta were too greedy and demanded too much. 'You are deep in debt,' they tell Al and Berta, 'but we know what we are doing and if you just renew this contract we will get your financial house in order.' Al and Berta sign on for another four years, but not without looking hard at some alternatives.*

Almost immediately after signing the deal, the advisers call Al and Berta in for a meeting. Their income will be cut; their fortune is gone and they are deeper in debt than anyone else in the neighbourhood. 'We must sell off whatever assets we can, cut costs, and tough it out. Things will get better in a few years. Feel free to talk to us. We listen. We care.'

The news is hard. Apparently, even after seven years of cuts their lifestyle is too high. In fact, the advisers now deny that any real cuts were ever made, and they show Al and Berta numbers indicating how much more they are getting now than before. Al and Berta remember things somehow differently, but the advisers are the ones with the figures.

Al and Berta and their children move back to the house they owned before their inheritance. Then the advisers ask them to sell their car and drive a second-hand sedan. There won't be any more holidays. The interest from the kids' trust fund must now be used to help pay off debt. It's a good thing Al and Berta kept their jobs.

As they look around the neighbourhood Al and Berta realize that, just like before the inheritance, their standard of living is barely average. Will the kids get to university? Will they ever buy a new car? At least the advisers offer to take a five percent reduction in their fees. Thank goodness for that.

As times go from hard to harder, though, Al and Berta start to study all those documents they had been given over the years by their advisers. Slowly they begin to see things differently. Time after time the decisions that got them into trouble were made by their advisers, not by them. It even looks like a lot of their money was invested with friends of their advisers. Al and Berta marvel at how badly their finances have been managed. How could enough money to keep a family in glory for generations be squandered so fast?

Their advisers continue to make even more cuts. As Al and Berta talk things over with their friends, they begin to doubt what their advisers are telling them. Their house isn't too fancy, as the advisers claim; in fact it needs more repairs than when they owned it years ago. The neighbours' cars are in nicer shape than their own (though the advisers claim otherwise), and their friends have better health insurance with much lower premiums. These advisers may be nice—sometimes Al and Berta even feel good when they tell them **bad** news. Even so, enough is enough.

The advisers sense this uneasiness. Shortly before their contract is up for its eighth consecutive renewal they tell Al and Berta that times are improving. The constraints have worked so well, it seems that Al and Berta can begin collecting more from their investments. Things are on track again, and it's time for some reinvestment. Al and Berta receive a cheque from the advisers' firm shortly before Christmas, with a cover note congratulating them for their patience, and telling them to be thankful they are in such good hands.

But instead of happiness the best thing Al and Berta feel is relief. Underlying this is a sense of resentment and irritation that sometimes simmers like quiet anger. The cheque from the firm is fine, but it's only a drop in the bucket. They still won't have enough to live like their neighbours. 'This wasn't our fault,' think Al and Berta, 'it was our advisers. Why should we be grateful to them?'

Al and Berta decide to themselves that next time they will not renew their advisers' contract. They decide it is time for a change.

12
THE SPECIAL
CASE OF
HEALTH CARE

WHILE ALBERTANS were being told the costs of health care were doubling (by the minister of health), or tripling (by the premier), government spending on health care had been declining in real terms for several years. More than anything else, health care has been the scapegoat that has paid the price for years of Tory mismanagement in other areas of government. This is not accidental. I will argue that there are compelling reasons that some people want to break the public health system.

When Don Getty resigned, Albertans had what might be considered an ideal health care system. The finest doctors, nurses, and other professionals worked in first-rate facilities with state-of-the-art equipment. Per capita costs had been contained for several years (adjusting for inflation). Systems were in place to insure spending would remain tightly controlled and efficiencies would improve. These included caps on total payments to physicians, and a hospital funding system that compared productivity among hospitals and rewarded the most efficient ones.

Today, Alberta's health care system is struggling and public confidence has fallen seriously. How poorly supported is health care in Alberta? There are many measures, and not all yield the same answer. But general patterns do emerge.

One common measure is the proportion of gross domestic product (GDP) a province spends on health care. This tells how much of its total wealth a society is spending on health. In Alberta's case, it has ranked last among the ten provinces in this category for years. In 1994, Statistics Canada figures say Alberta spent 7.9% of GDP on health care, compared to a Canadian average of 9.7% and an American rate of about 14%.[64] With the Klein government's cuts and Alberta's economic growth this already-low figure will drop sharply by the time the 1996 figures are available.

If the Klein government's announced plans for cuts were to be fully implemented, Alberta's 1996/97 per capita funding for health care would be 28% below the average of the other provinces with balanced budgets. For every dollar Alberta would spend, Newfoundland would spend $1.12, New Brunswick $1.27, Manitoba $1.33, and Saskatchewan $1.24.[65] With the government's plans for reinvestment, these figures no doubt overstate how low Alberta stands, but the figures give an unmistakable sense of how poorly supported Alberta's health care system has become in the hands of this government.

My own analysis of the data indicates that per capita funding of health care peaked in Alberta in

1987.[66] This is consistent with the government's internal data as shown in the graph on page 18, though my analysis shows a steeper decline in health-care expenditures.

I have never seen reliable data to support Ralph Klein's claims that in the years before he became premier, health care spending in Alberta had 'tripled,' or that costs were 'soaring,' 'skyrocketing,' or 'out of control.' *The premier's position cannot be defended with reliable data.* The government has played a cynical game of politics with health care, and in the process with people's jobs, health, and lives.

The excessiveness of the budget cuts turns up in many ways. For example, the government's target level for hospital beds was 2.4 beds per thousand residents. But a study conducted by a major consulting firm for the Capital Health Authority in 1996 found that in Edmonton, bed levels were already below that target before the major Klein government cuts began. By late 1995, bed levels had fallen almost 40% below the target, to 1.47 beds per thousand.[67] Reality outstripped political myth.

The 'reinvestment' program announced by the Minister of Health Halvar Jonson in November, 1996, was a tacit admission that the cuts had gone too far. But it continued to build political myth, for as was shown in 'Pulling the Wool,' above, health-care funding will not in fact regain lost ground through the reinvestment—it will continue to decline through the effects of inflation and population growth. Even with the proposed reinvestment, health care funding in Alberta in 1999 will be an estimated 27% lower in real terms than at the end of the Getty cuts in 1992.

The Klein government's 'reinvestment' in health care is a permanent crippling of Alberta's health system, a situation that will suit some people well.

• • •

With health care on the front pages and privatization in the back rooms, Alberta's health services are worth a special discussion.[68]

HEALTH CARE: PUBLIC OR PRIVATE?

If you called a policeman because your house was robbed and he said he wouldn't investigate unless you paid him, would that be right? Being required to buy police services when you need them is contrary to the basic integrity of a civil society. Some things should not be turned into products to be bought and sold. Judges are forbidden from administering justice according to who can pay. If teachers gave top marks to children whose parents paid them the most, the public education system would collapse along with our principle of equal opportunity. Civil servants are obliged to respond to every citizen equally and to refuse bribes.

In some places any of these things—policing, justice, education, government services—*can* be bought and sold. Any person knows this who has done business in some third-world countries, where payoffs to officials and under-the-table deals are routine. One difference between a corrupt and a civilized society is its ability to resist making everything a product for sale.

Canadians have decided that health care belongs among the services that are available to every citizen:

it is best not to turn health care into a commodity and put it up for sale. Unlike consumer goods, the rules of the free market do not work well with health care.

• • •

THE UNIQUE ECONOMICS OF HEALTH CARE

The economics of health care are unique because the forces controlling supply, demand, and prices are different for health care than for other goods and services. In the market for health care, the normal freedoms of the consumer do not apply.

The economics of free enterprise usually work well. If buyers and sellers of a product can do business as equals, and if there are enough sellers to insure competition and enough buyers that one or two cannot corner the market, everyone benefits. Even with a necessity of life like food, the system can work well: there are lots of farmers, restaurants and grocers, and everyone is a customer with foreseeable needs, so with a minimum of regulations things work to the best.

Health care is different. For one thing, my health is important to me in a way that consumer goods are not. I am separate from the things I own—my house, car, clothes—but my health or my sickness is part of me.

Health affects people to their core, as anyone with chronic pain or a debilitating disease will tell you. People need their health to get along in life in a way that they don't need many other things. To apply the economics that work for chocolate bars and sofa-beds to health care is a mistake for three reasons:

PEOPLE CAN'T EASILY CONTROL THEIR DEMAND FOR SERVICES. People do not generally control when they get sick, or with what ailment. They unexpectedly find themselves unwell, they may need help to get better, and their ability to make decisions for themselves may be hindered by their sickness. A car accident victim or a cancer patient looking for health care is in a very different position than someone looking for a replacement for a broken toaster.

IT IS DIFFICULT TO BE A WELL-INFORMED CONSUMER. 'Shopping around' is generally not encouraged (least of all by the government) and can be difficult or impossible, especially when one is sick. An even greater hurdle to becoming well-informed is the difficult technical knowledge it takes to understand many medical conditions. Few patients are in a position to judge for themselves which procedures or medications are best. And the consequences of a mistake can be disastrous.

COMPETITION IN HEALTH CARE IS UNLIKE COMPETITION WITH OTHER PRODUCTS. If I am shopping for shoes or groceries, there are many businesses competing to give me the best product at the lowest price. But competition doesn't work efficiently in health care. It is just not practical. Someone shopping for a car takes various models for a test drive. How can you test drive a cancer therapy? When you are having a heart attack or suspect your child has an ear infection, are you going to check with several doctors to see which will serve you best?

In a competitive market consumers often check things out before they buy them. With health care the product is often consumed before the patient knows if he or she is satisfied. You can't 'take back' a surgical operation or pills already swallowed. Neither are doctors and drug companies likely to promise 'full satisfaction or your money refunded.' Medicine simply holds too many uncertainties.

There is another problem with competition in health care. A wide-open market for health care can actually increase health problems and costs, not reduce them. It is often easier for health providers to expand their business by playing on the fears of consumers than by competing against one another. Convincing people they need health services even when they don't is good business, but not good health care.

In the United States, where there is wide-open competition, health-care providers often have 'sales.' Hospitals and doctors hold promotions on everything from hysterectomies to face lifts. It is in the interests of the health industry to increase the number of people who are, or fret that they might be, unhealthy. This has led to what some people call the 'diseasing of America.' And with increased competition, costs have gone up far faster than inflation.

This becomes a problem for health insurance companies, who face rising claims. They respond by restricting health-care coverage. Many US patients must now have their treatment determined by insurance companies rather than by their personal doctors.

The problems of private insurance for health care extend beyond the issue of insurance companies dictating medical treatment. Insurance companies make their profit by paying out as little as possible in claims, while charging as much as possible in premiums. In other words, for-profit health care insurance will tend to drive a health care system to the lowest services and the highest premiums. This problem was a central concern in Canada in the 1960s, and was a big reason that Canada committed to public health care insurance. Under the Canadian system, the intent is to provide the greatest benefits for the lowest cost.

As well, a single public insurance plan provides huge administrative efficiencies over a multitude of private insurers. It can eliminate duplication, standardize and reduce paperwork, and give the insurer the clout to negotiate firmly with doctors to control their expenses. In the United States, the administrative costs of the health care system are typically several times higher than in Canada.

All these factors make it impossible to apply free-market economics to health care. Not surprisingly, when a jurisdiction attempts to turn the health-care sector into a free market it creates a handful of big winners—the ones who can take advantage of the weak position of patients—and a truckload of big losers—the rest of us.

● ● ●

A common idea for reducing health-care costs is to charge user fees for hospitals and allow extra billing by doctors. Both of these have been tried from time to time in Canada—and in countries including Australia, Britain, and New Zealand—but they seldom have the desired effects.

User fees for hospitals, such as an admission fee, have little impact on hospital use. The decision to hospitalize someone is not determined simply by price—too many other factors take priority. Being admitted to hospital should be a medical decision, not a financial one. And though some argue that user fees can be a good source of revenue for hospitals, experience shows they are simply too small to make a big difference in rates of hospitalization. On top of that, the cost of collecting them can be almost as great as the income they provide.

If user fees for hospitals don't work, what about extra billing by doctors? Unfortunately, experience here is no better. Saskatchewan, for example, experimented with extra billing in the 1970s and found that the only people who reduced their use of the health care system were the poor and the elderly, often the ones who could least afford the extra costs but most needed the services. Other people didn't cut back at all, and physicians actually increased their billings. Alberta's experience with extra billing in the early 1980s was similar.

The burdens of user fees for hospitals and extra billing by physicians fall disproportionately on the sick, the elderly, and the poor. Wherever they have been tried, they have been practically useless in reducing health care costs or demands on doctors and hospitals. As with other attempts at turning health care into a free market, they are flawed from the beginning.

HOW DOES PRIVATE HEALTH CARE UNDERMINE PUBLIC HEALTH CARE?

During radio broadcasts of sporting events in the winter of 1996, listeners in Alberta often heard an ad for a private, for-profit, magnetic-resonance-imaging clinic. The biggest selling feature of the ads was that a person could get an MRI scan immediately at this clinic while, as the ad itself made clear, waiting lists at public facilities could be several months.

The most important point here is this: if it weren't for line-ups in the public health system, the private magnetic-resonance centre would probably be out of business. Who would pay hundreds of dollars for a service they could get just as quickly without a charge?

If the public health care system is working well there is almost no market for a private system. So as a matter of survival, the private system must do what it can to prevent the public system from functioning at its best.

If anyone thinks this is an overstatement, consider what happened in the United States during Bill Clinton's first term in office. In 1992, he was elected president largely on the strength of his promise to reform the health care system. Health care was a top worry for American voters. Costs were soaring and it was one of the biggest, fastest growing industries in the country, surpassing the massive US defense industry. By the early 1990s, the US health industry reached an annual volume of $840 billion (US), about the size of the entire economy of Great Britain. It was serving its financial backers very well, but it wasn't serving ordinary Americans: tens of millions had no health coverage, and tens of millions more had insufficient coverage. All this in a system that costs almost double what Alberta's 'out-of-control' system costs, in terms of GDP.

But the massive US health industry was deeply opposed to reforms. In the decade before Clinton was elected, it spent more than $60 million (US) lobbying the US Congress. This investment paid off. Within six weeks of his election victory, Clinton had backed away from major reforms, concluding it was impossible to overcome the health industry lobby.

Private for-profit health care combines three of our society's most powerful interest groups: doctor's, insurance companies, and drug companies. Many in these groups believe that their business survival demands a for-profit system. In fact, drug companies now own many US medical clinics and health maintenance organizations.[69] When they are working together, the ability of these three groups to campaign for a weaker public health care system can seem irresistible, as the American public has learned.

• • •

When the cutbacks started, the Klein government dismissed people with problems as 'whiners' and 'victims of the week.' But the evidence of serious trouble in Alberta's health-care system is now too common and serious to be ignored.

It has become routine for problems with Alberta's health-care system to make media headlines. Neurosurgeons, obstetricians, pediatricians, psychiatrists and many others have been leaving the province.

Rural areas cannot recruit doctors. There are long delays for service, and staff are under unprecedented stress. Facilities are closed, waiting lists are long, equipment is worn out, and thousands of jobs are cut. A major survey sponsored by the government's own Department of Health reveals that among people who have fair or poor health—those who use and need health services the most—a majority rate the health system as only poor or fair.[70]

The cutbacks to Alberta's health care system were not driven by financial need. As the government's own financial evidence confirms, health costs were under control long before Mr. Klein became premier.

But there are other possible reasons the cuts were made. A phrase sometimes used by the government's Public Affairs Officers when they plan a public relations campaign is, 'Who will be mad, and who will be glad?' It is obvious who is mad over the health cuts. But who could be glad?

These cuts were driven by greed and by ideology.

It should be clear where the greed comes in. A health-care system operating without adequate funding does benefit some people. As the MRI ad suggests, supporters of private clinics of all kinds are glad when the public system breaks down because it creates a market for them. Proposals from private companies to reopen public hospitals, including small rural hospitals and the Grace Hospital in Calgary, are serious symptoms of underlying threats to Alberta's health-care system.

The greed at the heart of private health care is often justified by ideology. It has become ideology for some people that public services are always ineffective and inefficient. Public services are indeed sometimes ineffective and inefficient. But in health care the evidence shows the public sector works best, and for good reasons of economics.

Justice Emmett Hall, who was instrumental in designing the Canadian medicare system in the mid-1960s, was asked by the federal government to review it in the late 1970s. His words are as relevant today as when he tabled his report:

> *Canadians...as a society, are aware that the trauma of illness, the pain of surgery, the slow decline to death, are burdens enough for the human being to bear without the added burden of medical or hospital bills penalizing the patient at the moment of vulnerability. The Canadian people determined that they should band together to pay medical bills and hospital bills when they were well and income earning. Health services were no longer items to be bought off the shelf and paid for at the checkout stand. Nor was their price to be bargained for at the time they are sought. They were a fundamental need, like education, which Canadians could meet collectively and pay for through taxes.*[71]

13
THE ACID TEST

THE ACID TEST of every government is to ask, 'Are we better off or worse off than when the government was elected?' After 25 years of one-party government in Alberta, this isn't just the big question, it is the only question. Here is some evidence to judge:

- Alberta has gone from having the finest public services in Canada to having some of the poorest. Alberta ranks at or near the bottom of the ten provinces in support for most public services, even after 'reinvestment' proposals.[72]

- More than $80 billion in non-renewable resource revenues has flowed through Alberta government coffers since the Progressive Conservatives were first elected: far, far more than in any other province in Canada. A very small fraction of it sits in the Heritage Trust Fund. The rest is gone forever.

- Alberta has piled up a multi-billion-dollar debt (estimates of the size of the debt vary widely, even using the government's own figures).[73] Even with a rapid repayment schedule it will be years before the smallest estimate of the debt—the so-called 'net debt'—is paid down.

- In Alberta today, the assets that offset and justify the debt (as one justifies a mortgage by enjoying a house) are quickly eroding. For example, the province's physical assets—including roads, sidewalks, sewers, and public buildings (hospitals, schools, universities)—are in rapid decline.[74]

- Alberta has developed the most heavily subsidized private sector in Canada. The proportion of the provincial budget spent on industrial development has doubled since the Progressive Conservatives first came to power. The government has routinely spent more on industrial development than it collects in corporate taxes.

- Alberta's conventional oil reserves have been depleted to less than half their peak levels. By the time a baby born in 1996 graduates from high school, Alberta's era as a significant conventional oil producer will have ended. Natural gas reserves will last longer, but they are also declining. While the oil sands will last indefinitely, they supply only a small portion of Alberta's petroleum royalties because of high production costs and low royalty rates.

- Alberta society is fractured. Haves and have-nots blame one another for social problems and government decisions. Rural areas are pitted against the cities, and the cities are played against each other. Public workers, doctors, nurses, and teachers are portrayed as self-serving. People who speak out are degraded as whiners. Social unity has been sacrificed to the politics of divide and conquer.

Twenty-five years ago Alberta was solid and Albertans were secure. There were huge oil and gas reserves; education, health and other programs that led the nation; sound government finances; and a promising and certain future. In recent years Alberta has been hollowed out, a shell of its former self.

• • •

All too often, democratic governments born from good intentions die from addiction to power. Idealism gives way to cynicism, openness is overwhelmed by manipulation, the high moral ground is undermined by the lust for glory and self-interest. The narcotic effect of command comes to glaze the eyes of leaders, sharpening their wits but dulling their souls. Nothing matters more than staying at the centre of attention, wealth, and control.

After 25 years of unbroken one-party rule in Alberta, good intentions have gradually and inevitably gone bad.

Political leaders alone cannot determine the public culture of a society. But they can influence it strongly. They can appeal to the anxious, selfish, mean-spirited nature that lurks in each of us, or they can appeal to nobility, tolerance, and generosity. People with differing points of view can be sincerely considered, or they can be called humiliating names. Governments can help people get a fair break and build a better society, or they can further enrich and empower those who are already rich and powerful, building a society of haves and have-nots. Governments can tell the truth, or they can lie.

TABLE A **The Unprecedented Scale of Private Sector Subsidies in Alberta**

Year	Total Spending by Alberta Government on Resource Conservation & Industrial Development *(Millions)*	Per Capita Spending by Alberta Government on Resource Conservation & Industrial Development *(Constant 1994 $)*	Per Capita Spending on Resource Conservation & Industrial Development by Alberta Government, as a % of Average of All Other Canadian Provinces
1971	$64	$152	131%
1972	$73	$163	126%
1973	$70	$143	113%
1974	$112	$203	164%
1975	$207	$330	210%
1976	$257	$367	202%
1977	$521	$654	369%
1978	$510	$557	304%
1979	$711	$696	352%
1980	$776	$663	328%
1981	$905	$651	295%
1982	$1376	$857	406%
1983	$2784	$1634	805%
1984	$2492	$1437	678%
1985	$2502	$1383	609%
1986	$2999	$1594	620%
1987	$3013	$1526	644%
1988	$2332	$1145	559%
1989	$2083	$963	393%
1990	$2047	$882	317%
1991	$1893	$755	312%
1992	$2073	$801	274%
1993	$2159	$814	334%
1994	$1727	$636	273%

Source: Consumer Price Index, all-items (Alberta 1978-1994; Edmonton 1971-1977). Resource Conservation and Industrial Development figures from Statistics Canada Cansim databases, updated January 1996.

This table provides a good indication of the Alberta government's spending on private sector subsidies. It is based on a Statistics Canada tabulation from provincial public accounts. Statistics Canada calls this category 'Resource Conservation and Industrial Development,' which is defined elsewhere in a footnote. The startling growth of spending under the 25-year administration of the Progressive Conservatives is clear. The amount spent grew 1000% from 1971 to the period stretching from 1983 to 1987, even after inflation and population growth are considered. While it declined markedly from this peak, in 1994 it was still four times the level of when the Tories came to power (accounting for inflation and population growth).

A different indicator of the high scale of spending in this area is the comparison with the average for the rest of Canada, shown in the column furthest right. Compared to the rest of the country, Alberta's subsidies reached remarkable heights, exceeding the average for the rest of Canada by 500% to 800% every year from 1983 to 1988. In 1994, they still remained at well over double the average rate of the other provinces.

While a certain level of support for the private sector is justifiable, the wide fluctuation and very high levels in Alberta suggest that this spending has more to do with politics and power than with sound economics or the relatively fixed costs of infrastructure such as petroleum regulation.

Natural Resource Revenues in Alberta and Canada

Year	Total Natural Resource Revenues Received by Alberta Government *(Millions)*	Per Capita Natural Resource Revenues Received by Alberta Government *(Constant 1994 $)*	Per Capita Natural Resource Revenues Received by All Other Governments in Canada *(Constant 1994 $)*
1971	$247	$604	$75
1972	$288	$661	$71
1973	$352	$738	$80
1974	$610	$1131	$102
1975	$1407	$2295	$140
1976	$1785	$2598	$110
1977	$2214	$2834	$99
1978	$3258	$3617	$121
1979	$4053	$4034	$141
1980	$4731	$4099	$180
1981	$5153	$3756	$175
1982	$5232	$3297	$110
1983	$5257	$3120	$106
1984	$5704	$3324	$128
1985	$6032	$3370	$130
1986	$5668	$3042	$125
1987	$2703	$1382	$91
1988	$3605	$1787	$105
1989	$2837	$1323	$117
1990	$2946	$1280	$112
1991	$3289	$1321	$97
1992	$2554	$995	$84
1993	$2656	$1009	$89
1994	$3263	$1211	$115
Totals	$75.8 billion	$52,829	$2705

As the price of oil soared after 1973, so did the natural resource revenues received by the Alberta government. By 1975 Albertans were receiving 10 times the revenues from natural resources as other Canadians per person, and in some years in the 1980s this reached 30 times the average per capita level of other Canadians. From 1971 to 1994, resource revenues received by the Alberta government were worth $75.8 billion; adding estimates for 1995 and 1996, this reaches about $81 billion. This is about twice the total amount received by all other Canadians combined.

During this period the Alberta government received the equivalent in 1994 dollars of $53,000 per Albertan, or $212,000 for a family of four. All this money is from non-renewable resources, and almost all of it is gone.

This table shows revenues received from the sale of natural resources by a) the Government of Alberta, and b) all other governments (provincial, federal, territorial, municipal) in Canada. The table covers the 25 years since the Progressive Conservatives were first elected in Alberta. It also shows these same revenues per person in Alberta and in the rest of Canada, adjusted for inflation to 1994 dollars. The source of the information is Statistics Canada Cansim database, updated January 1996. Inflation adjustments are based on all-items consumer price indexes.

T A B L E   C   Resource Conservation and Industrial Development *(Thousands $)*

	1986/87	1987/88	1988/89	1989/90	1990/91	1991/92	1992/93	Total
Alberta								
Agriculture	729,881	603,601	635,602	755,443	723,411	1,043,009	1,175,654	5,666,601
Fish & Game	23,644	22,604	22,382	27,198	28,907	31,457	33,468	189,660
Forests	98,593	109,464	113,933	111,643	140,452	117,001	115,320	806,406
Mines, Oil, Gas	1,641,111	1,022,031	704,520	707,789	603,688	531,617	432,216	5,642,972
Tourism	23,330	26,133	36,622	42,854	46,547	40,800	33,937	250,223
Trade & Industry	134,911	110,215	196,415	130,806	134,694	93,411	135,858	936,310
Water Power	2616	2457	2655	2264	2299	2354	2439	17,084
Other	448,938	384,640	366,484	269,099	212,998	213,629	230,147	2,125,935
Total	3,103,024	2,281,145	2,078,613	2,047,096	1,892,996	2,073,278	2,159,039	15,635,191
Non-Agric. Total	2,373,143	1,677,544	1,443,011	1,291,653	1,169,585	1,030,269	983,385	9,968,590

Source: Statistics Canada special runs, July-August 1996, using Alberta Public Accounts. More recent figures unavailable at time of publication.

T A B L E D **Subsidies by the Alberta and
Saskatchewan Governments to the
'Mines, Oil, and Gas' Industries**

(Dollar figures are in millions.)

	1986/87	87/88	88/89	89/90	90/91	91/92	92/93
Alberta	$1641	$1,022	$704	$707	$604	$532	$432
Saskatchewan	$23	$20	$17	$19	$15	$174	$7

Here are the comparative levels of subsidies by the Alberta and
Saskatchewan governments to the 'Mines, Oil, and Gas' industry
(overwhelmingly oil and gas) compiled by Statistics Canada from
provincial public accounts. More recent figures at this level of detail
are not available.

T A B L E E **Subsidies by the Alberta and British
Columbia Governments to the
Tourism Industry**

(Dollar figures are in millions.)

	1986/87	87/88	88/89	89/90	90/91	91/92	92/93
Alberta	$23	$26	$37	$43	$47	$41	$34
B.C.	$19	$34	$36	$20	$20	$14	$14

Here are the comparative levels of subsidies by Alberta and British
Columbia in the 'Tourism' category compiled by Statistics Canada
from provincial public accounts. More recent figures at this level of
detail are not available.

Spending on Health Care by the Alberta Government

Year	Total Spending on Health Care by Alberta Government (Millions)	Per Capita Spending on Health Care by Alberta Government (Constant 1994 $)	Per Capita Spending as a % of 1986 (Inflation Adjusted)	Spending on Health Care as a % of Total Alberta Government Expenditures
1981	$1601	$1234	74%	23%
1982	$2015	$1314	79%	23%
1983	$2616	$1572	95%	21%
1984	$2878	$1670	101%	23%
1985	$2870	$1619	97%	23%
1986	$3102	$1660	100%	23%
1987	$3332	$1702	102%	23%
1988	$3186	$1560	94%	23%
1989	$3324	$1541	93%	23%
1990	$3516	$1524	92%	23%
1991	$3764	$1488	90%	23%
1992	$3987	$1518	91%	24%

Source: Statistics Canada Cansim database, updated January 1996. Inflation adjustment uses the health services consumer price index for Alberta, produced by Statistics Canada.

This table shows my own analysis of trends in spending on health care by the Alberta government from 1981 to 1992, the decade preceding the election of Ralph Klein as Premier. An analysis of this table provides results consistent with the government's own internal studies, as well as with various other studies, though not at all consistent with the political claims of the Klein government. The second column of figures shows per capita spending after accounting for inflation (in 1994 dollars). This peaks in 1987 and then declines by 11% in the next five years. Throughout this entire period, health care spending takes a consistent 23% or 24% of total provincial spending.

NOTES

1 For example: 'The Report of the Critical Assessment Committee,
Region 10 Medical Staff', released October 22, 1996, provides at
least two examples of deaths that resulted from conditions created by the health cuts. On August 6, 1996, the Chief of
Anesthesia of the Royal Alexandra Hospital in Edmonton
resigned, describing situations in which patients were dying
needlessly due to cutbacks (*Edmonton Journal*, August 7, 1996, p
A1). On August 14, 1996, the Leader of the Opposition, Grant
Mitchell, listed in the Legislature the names of nine people, and
tabled the names of over forty, who had 'died or suffered needlessly' as a result of health care cuts (*Alberta Hansard*, August 14,
1996, p 2133).

What is remarkable about these examples is that it is difficult
to prove conclusively that deaths were caused by political decisions, and to then make this publicly known. First, there is the
need to respect patient confidentiality, and the reluctance of families to become involved in the media and political debates that
speaking out requires. Second, there are legal risks, including law-
suits, that may result for hospitals, doctors, and staff who admit
that deaths occurred unnecessarily. Finally, cutbacks to services
resulting from cutbacks to funding may not cause deaths immediately and directly, while still creating conditions that lead to
unnecessary suffering or death. Given these considerations, I
have no doubt that the actual number of people who have died
unnecessarily due to health cuts is much higher than will ever be
known publicly.

2 From 1973 to 1982, I was a member of the Health Facilities
Review Committee. This committee, appointed by cabinet, is
responsible for reviewing the operations of all hospitals, nursing
homes, lodges, and other health facilities in Alberta. It reports
through the Minister of Health to the Legislative Assembly. My

three-year appointment to this committee was renewed twice by cabinet. During 1981–82, I was also appointed by cabinet to serve as a member of the Nursing Home Review Panel. This panel reviewed the entire nursing home system in Alberta, visiting all nursing homes and holding public and private hearings. It submitted its report to the provincial government in 1982. In addition I served as a public servant and as a consultant. My work on the seniors report described here was three days a week for 20 months.

3   Eight days after the June 15, 1993, general election, the Tories signed a $100 million loan guarantee with Bovar, the company operating the Swan Hills Waste Treatment Plant. When the Liberals revealed this story the Tories denied it was a new loan guarantee, but the acting Auditor-General for the Province eventually confirmed that it was new (*Edmonton Journal*, September 30, 1994, p A7). Later that same summer, the Tories provided a $1 million loan guarantee to Beatrice Foods to construct a cookie factory (*Edmonton Journal*, September 2, 1993, p B1). During this period the Tories also provided a $50 million loan guarantee extension to Canadian Airlines, a decision which they openly acknowledged and initially claimed was the 'one exception' to their policy of no loan guarantees (*Edmonton Journal*, July 24, 1993, p B8).

4   Melville L. McMillan, 'Leading the Way of Missing the Mark? The Klein Government's Fiscal Plan,' Western Centre for Economic Research, University of Alberta, Edmonton, 1996.

5   The briefing package was prepared with the involvement of various departments, particularly Treasury, Health, and Education. There were several graphs in this package in addition to the two shown here, covering many aspects of deficit financing, debt growth, revenues, and expenditures. The expenditure graphs focused on education and health. While the graphs I have included here are reliable, some graphs in the package were misleading. For example, one showed costs for health care rising sharply into the future, based apparently on an unsupported extrapolation of the high rates of inflation of the 1980s into the late 1990s.

6   Thomas J. Courchene, *Social Canada in the Millennium* (Toronto: C.D. Howe Institute, 1994), p 180.

7   Melville L. McMillan, 'Leading the Way of Missing the Mark? The Klein Government's Fiscal Plan,' Western Centre for Economic Research, University of Alberta, Edmonton, 1996.

8   I have used many sources for the discussion in this chapter, including the annual reports of the Alberta Departments of Energy and of Economic Development; various Treasury Department reports, especially the Budget Addresses of 1991 and 1992; media coverage throughout the period by the *Edmonton Journal* and *Alberta Report*; and the following books and articles: Andrew Nikiforuk, Sheila Pratt, and Don Wanagas, *Running on Empty*, (Edmonton: NeWest Press, 1987); Thomas J. Courchene, *Social Canada in the Millennium* (Toronto: C.D. Howe Institute, 1994), p 180; Melville L. McMillan, 'Leading the Way of Missing the Mark? The Klein Government's Fiscal Plan,' Western Centre for Economic Research, University of Alberta, Edmonton, 1996; Melville L. McMillan and Allan Warrack, 'Alberta's Fiscal Update: One-Track (Thinking) Towards Deficit Reduction,' Western Centre for Economic Research, University of Alberta, Edmonton, 1995; Allan Tupper, Larry Pratt and Ian Urquhart, 'The Role of Government,' in *Government and Politics in Alberta*, Allan Tupper and Roger Gibbins, eds. (Edmonton: University of Alberta Press, 1992).

9   *Alberta Report*, August 1, 1988.

10 *Edmonton Journal*, October 14, 1992.

11 Melville L. McMillan and Allan Warrack, 'Alberta's Fiscal Update: One-Track (Thinking) Towards Deficit Reduction,' Western Centre for Economic Research, University of Alberta, Edmonton, 1995.

12 *Alberta Hansard*, April 4, 1991.

13 *Alberta Hansard*, April 13, 1992.

14 Records of attendance at Legislative Sessions kept by the Clerk of the Legislature confirm that both Ralph Klein and Jim Dinning were present when both statements were made by Johnston.

15 *Edmonton Journal*, June 18, 1994.

16 *Edmonton Journal*, December 3, 1996, p A1, quoting the premier on an open-line radio show.

17 *Edmonton Journal*, May 11, 1995, p A7.

18 *Edmonton Journal*, May 23, 1996, p A5.

19 Alberta's spending on health care by 1996 is well under 8% of

GNP, the lowest rate in Canada. The rate in the United States is about 14% [Joan Price Boase, *Canadian-American Public Policy* (Orono: The Canadian-American Center, University of Maine, 1996), p 3].

20 *Edmonton Journal*, November 26, 1996, p A10; November 8, 1996, p A6.

21 Melville L. McMillan, 'Leading the Way of Missing the Mark? The Klein Government's Fiscal Plan,' Western Centre for Economic Research, University of Alberta, Edmonton, 1996; and Melville L. McMillan and Allan Warrack, 'Alberta's Fiscal Update: One-Track (Thinking) Towards Deficit Reduction,' Western Centre for Economic Research, University of Alberta, Edmonton, 1995.

22 Melville L. McMillan, 'Leading the Way of Missing the Mark? The Klein Government's Fiscal Plan,' Western Centre for Economic Research, University of Alberta, Edmonton, 1996.

23 'Patient Care in Region 10: Registered Nurses' Professional Concerns and Solutions,' Staff Nurses Association of Alberta, November 6, 1996, p 3.

24 Melville L. McMillan, 'Leading the Way of Missing the Mark? The Klein Government's Fiscal Plan,' Western Centre for Economic Research, University of Alberta, Edmonton, 1996.

25 Alberta Department of Education, *Annual Report 1995–96*, Appendix B.

26 'Patient Care in Region 10: Registered Nurses' Professional Concerns and Solutions,' Staff Nurses Association of Alberta, November 6, 1996, p 5, citing figures from Alberta Health.

27 Southam News/CBC News, *Eyes on Alberta*, March, 1995.

28 *Edmonton Journal*, April 25, 1996, p A1.

29 Alberta Health 'Action on Health' advertisement, November 27, 1996, *Edmonton Journal*; and *Edmonton Journal*, November 26, 1996, pp A1, A3.

30 Melville L. McMillan, 'Leading the Way of Missing the Mark? The Klein Government's Fiscal Plan,' Western Centre for Economic Research, University of Alberta, Edmonton, 1996, p 14.

31 *Edmonton Journal*, May 11, 1996, p A10.

32 *Alberta Hansard*, May 14 and 15, 1996, and *Edmonton Senior*, June 1996, p 1.

33 *Calgary Herald*, May 15, 1996, p A13.

34 The research for this chapter and the next has been done in coop-

eration with Prof. David Cooper, Department of Accounting and Management Information Systems, Faculty of Business, University of Alberta, and draws on special computer runs done for the researchers by Statistics Canada.

35 See Table A.

36 The figure for income support is the amount under Vote 2.2 of Family and Social Services in the 1994–95 Public Accounts of the Province of Alberta. It includes payments to individuals and families, training, and a wide range of other services. It does not include income support to the handicapped or seniors. My figures for industrial development spending are based on Statistics Canada figures. The Alberta Public Accounts do not adequately consolidate all spending on industrial development; they distribute subsidies under various programs and net out some subsidies, such as the Royalty Tax Credit, before totals are compiled.

37 A simple way to track industrial development expenditures is to use Statistics Canada data on 'Resource Conservation and Industrial Development.' These show spending 'pertaining to the conservation and development of natural resources and the development and promotion of the processing, manufacturing, service and tourism industries.' They include direct government payments to corporations, tax breaks, losses on loan guarantees, research, marketing support, and a wide range of related items. They cover agriculture; mining, oil and gas; tourism; forestry; fish and game; trade and industry; water power; and 'other.' Statistics Canada cannot separate 'Resource Conservation' from 'Industrial Development.' Because all areas relate ultimately to the commercial use of resources and industrial development, I simply refer to them as 'Industrial Development.' This category does not include spending on environmental issues.

38 Andrew Nikiforuk, Sheila Pratt, and Don Wanagas, *Running on Empty*, (Edmonton: NeWest Press, 1987), p 149.

39 In fiscal 1987/88, 1988/89, and 1990/91, spending on 'resource conservation and industrial development' exceeded Alberta's annual deficits. Source: Statistics Canada Cansim database, updated January, 1996.

40 See Table B.

41 The 1994–95 Public Accounts place the total value of the Heritage Trust Fund at $11.9 billion, of which at least $2.4 billion are

invested in other branches of the government, such as social
housing, which arguably inflates the stated value of the fund.

42 These figures are based on estimates by the Canadian Association
of Petroleum Producers and the National Energy Board, cited in
Western Report, June 5, 1995, pp 12–13, and on Statistics Canada
data.

43 Statistics Canada Cansim database, updated January, 1996.

44 Statistics Canada Cansim database, updated January, 1996.

45 See Table C.

46 The 1994–95 Alberta Public Accounts show total expenditures of
$14.894 billion, and total corporate income tax revenue of $1.073
billion. Statistics Canada detailed calculations of Resource
Conservation and Industrial Development spending for fiscal
1994/95 were not available at time of publication of this book, but
extrapolating from the downward trend in this area in 1992/93
and 1993/94, I estimate non-agricultural spending at $889 million.
Subtracting this from corporate tax revenue provides net revenue
of $184 million, or slightly over 1% of total provincial expendi-
tures. I have not included agricultural subsidies or tax revenues.

I have not netted out fees and levies charged to the corporate
sector in this discussion of corporate taxes, nor do I net out health
and social insurance fees and levies paid by individuals in my dis-
cussions of health and social spending. Health and social
insurance levies, including health insurance premiums, appear
(based on a preliminary review of Statistics Canada data and
Alberta Public Accounts) to total far more than is levied to the corporate sector for services. Netting fees and levies out across all
spending areas—in other words, subtracting revenues from their
directly related expenditures—would have the greatest impact on
health spending, reducing expenditures to a markedly lower level.

47 *Edmonton Journal*, November 18, 1996, p C3.

48 *Edmonton Journal*, September 9, 1996, p A7.

49 See Table C.

50 Allan Tupper, Larry Pratt, and Ian Urquhart, 'The Role of
Government,' in *Government and Politics in Alberta*, Allan Tupper
and Roger Gibbins, eds. (Edmonton: University of Alberta Press,
1992), p 40.

51 *Energy Statistics Handbook.* Statistics Canada, Ottawa, May 1996, Table 4.13.

52 See Table D.

53 *1994–95 Alberta Consolidated Public Accounts, Vol. 2,* pp 126, 65, 55–59.

54 See Table E.

55 Statistics Canada Cansim database, updated January, 1996.

56 *Edmonton Journal,* November 28, 1996, p A3.

57 Cited in Michel Foucault, *Discipline and Punish* (New York: Vintage Books, 1979), pp 102–103.

58 Kenneth Whyte, 'Klein of the Times,' in *Saturday Night,* May, 1994, p 78.

59 *A Better Way: A Plan for Securing Alberta's Future,* Government of Alberta, February 24, 1994.

60 *Edmonton Journal,* September 26, 1996, p A7.

61 Peter Drucker, *The Practice of Management,* (New York: Harper and Row, 1954), p 37.

62 The literature on the importance of narratives in social life is immense, and a lot of work is being done in narrative psychology. Two good books in this area are: Jerome Bruner, *Actual Minds, Possible Worlds* (Cambridge, Massachusetts: Harvard University Press, 1986); and Theodore R. Sarbin, *Narrative Psychology: The Storied Nature of Human Conduct* (New York: Praeger Publishers, 1986).

63 Here I draw on Christopher Lasch's discussion of propaganda in *Culture of Narcissism* (New York: Norton, 1991), pp 76–77.

64 Statistics Canada National Health Expenditures, 1975–1994, Table 27. The American figure is from Joan Price Boase, *Health Care Reform or Health Care Rationing: A Comparative Study,* (Orono: The Canadian-American Center, The University of Maine, 1996).

65 Melville L. McMillan, 'Leading the Way of Missing the Mark? The Klein Government's Fiscal Plan,' Western Centre for Economic Research, University of Alberta, Edmonton, 1996.

66 See Table F.

67 'Health Care System Benchmarking,' Project Report, KPMG Consultants, March 29, 1996. This study is worth careful review,

for it indicates the extremes to which the Klein cuts have led the health care system in many categories when compared to other jurisdictions in Canada, Britain, and New Zealand.

68 My discussion on health care draws on a wide range of sources, some of which are cited in other chapters. On the US health care system the following were important sources: Spyrus Andreopoulous, ed., *National Health Insurance: Can We Learn From Canada?* (New York: John Wiley and Sons, 1975); Joan Price Boase, *Health Care Reform or Health Care Rationing: A Comparative Study* (Orono: The Canadian-American Center, The University of Maine, 1996); Theodore Marmor, *Understanding Health Care Reform*, (New Haven: Yale University Press, 1994); Nancy McKenzie, ed., *Beyond Crisis* (New York: Meridian Press, 1994); J.A. Morone and G.S. Belklin, eds., *The Politics of Health Care Reform* (London: Duke University Press, 1994).

On the Canadian health care system the following were useful sources: 'Reality Check,' Alberta Medical Association, Edmonton, 1996; Robin R. Badgley and R. David Smith, *User Charges for Health Services*, The Ontario Council of Health, Toronto, 1979; M.L. Barer, R.G. Evans, and G.L. Stoddart, *Controlling Health Care Costs by Direct Charges to Patients: Snare or Delusion?*, Ontario Economic Council, Toronto, 1979; B. Singh Bolaria and Harley D. Dickinson, eds., *Sociology of Health Care in Canada* (Toronto: Harcourt Brace Jovanovich, 1988); Donna Wilson, ed., *The Canadian Health Care System* (Edmonton: Health Canada/University of Alberta, 1995).

69 For example, the June, 1996, cover story of *Harper's Magazine* points out that SmithKline Beecham, one of the world's largest drug companies, has bought a large number of medical clinics in the U.S. and now owns a system that covers 6000 doctors and their patients. The article argues that this is part of a much larger trend, and is contributing to a backlash against managed care in the US (Greg Critser, 'Oh, How Happy We Will Be,' in *Harper's Magazine*, June 1996, pp 39–48).

70 *The 1996 Public Survey about Health and the Health System in Alberta*, conducted by the Population Research Laboratory, University of Alberta, for Alberta Health, May, 1996. For an interesting analysis of this compare the government press release about the survey, with the headline 'Albertans Remain Confident

in Health System According to Survey,' with a guest column in the *Edmonton Journal* by Richard Fraser, 'Survey of Sick Albertans Disturbing,' November 8, 1996, p A19.

71 Emmett M. Hall, *Canada's National-Provincial Health Program for the 1980s*, Department of National Health and Welfare, 1980, p 6.

72 Melville L. McMillan, 'Leading the Way of Missing the Mark? The Klein Government's Fiscal Plan,' Western Centre for Economic Research, University of Alberta, Edmonton, 1996.

73 For example, Mark Lisac, Provincial Affairs Columnist for the *Edmonton Journal*, uses government information to report a net debt of $6.2 billion; an 'unmatured debt' of $22.1 billion; a 'direct unmatured debt' of $17.7 billion which was close to zero in 1985; and a 'gross debt' of $32.1 billion. (*Edmonton Journal*, November 12, 1996, p A10).

74 For example, see *Fiscal Impact of Provincial Restructuring on Urban Municipalities*, Alberta Urban Municipalities Association, September, 1996, documenting an average 52% reduction in provincial funding to municipalities, and the effect of this on rapidly deteriorating roads, walks, and lighting.

ABOUT THE AUTHOR

KEVIN TAFT grew up in Alberta, and first became involved with the provincial government as a high school student in 1973, shortly after the Progressive Conservatives were first elected. He worked in a variety of capacities with or near the provincial government for many years through the 1970s, 1980s, and early 1990s. He is now completing a PhD in Business through the University of Warwick in England. He lives in Alberta with his wife and two sons.

ABOUT PARKLAND INSTITUTE

PARKLAND INSTITUTE is a non-profit research network that conducts, promotes, and disseminates research in the broad tradition of Canadian political economy. The Institute operates under the auspices of the Faculty of Arts, University of Alberta, with input from academic members, as well as from church, private sector, union, professional, community and general members drawn from across Alberta.

For more copies of *Shredding the Public Interest*, please check with your local bookseller. If you have no local bookseller, please order from:

UBC Press
6344 Memorial Road
Vancouver, BC
V6T 1Z2
Toll-free fax orders: 1-800-668-0821
Customer Service: (604) 822-5959
E-mail: orders@ubcpress.ubc.ca

For more information, or for a complete catalogue, please call or write to:

The University of Alberta Press
141 Athabasca Hall
Edmonton, Alberta
T6G 2E8
Tel: (403) 492-3662
Fax: (403) 492-0719
E-mail: uap@gpu.srv.ualberta.ca
Internet: www.quasar.ualberta.ca/press

Community associations may order *Shredding the Public Interest* in bulk by calling or writing to:

Parkland Institute
University of Alberta
11044–90 Ave.
Edmonton, Alberta
T6G 2E1
Tel: (403) 492-8558
Fax: (403) 492-8738
E-mail: parkland@gpu.srv.ualberta.ca
Internet: www.ualberta.ca/˜parkland/homepage